# Adolf Hitler

# Titles in the
# People Who Made History Series

Charles Darwin
Adolf Hitler
John F. Kennedy
Martin Luther King Jr.

# Adolf Hitler

Brenda Stalcup, *Book Editor*

David L. Bender, *Publisher*
Bruno Leone, *Executive Editor*
Bonnie Szumski, *Editorial Director*
David M. Haugen, *Managing Editor*
Scott Barbour, *Series Editor*

Greenhaven Press, Inc., San Diego, CA

Every effort has been made to trace the owners of copyrighted material. The articles in this volume may have been edited for content, length, and/or reading level. The titles have been changed to enhance the editorial purpose. Those interested in locating the original source will find the complete citation on the first page of each article.

Library of Congress Cataloging-in-Publication Data

Adolf Hitler / Brenda Stalcup, book editor.
    p.    cm. — (People who made history)
    Includes bibliographical references and index.
    ISBN 0-7377-0223-0 (alk. paper). —
ISBN 0-7377-0222-2 (pbk. : alk. paper)
    1. Hitler, Adolf, 1889–1945. 2. Germany—Politics and government—1933–1945. 3. National socialism. 4. Heads of state—Germany Biography. 5. Holocaust, Jewish (1939–1945)—Causes. I. Stalcup, Brenda. II. Series.
DD247.H5A7578    2000
943.086'092—dc21                99-36361
[B]                               CIP

Cover photo: Archive Photos
National Archives, 23

Copyright ©2000 by Greenhaven Press, Inc.
PO Box 289009
San Diego, CA 92198-9009
Printed in the U.S.A.

# CONTENTS

ing his speeches in order to more effectively sway his
listeners.

## Chapter 3: Hitler, World War II, and the Holocaust

to different parts of the world. The idea of establishing death camps in which to kill the European Jews was a later development.

# Chapter 4: The Historical Significance of Adolf Hitler

# FOREWORD

In the vast and colorful pageant of human history, a handful of individuals stand out. They are the men and women who have come variously to be called "great," "leading," "brilliant," "pivotal," or "infamous" because they and their deeds forever changed their own society or the world as a whole. Some were political or military leaders—kings, queens, presidents, generals, and the like—whose policies, conquests, or innovations reshaped the maps and futures of countries and entire continents. Among those falling into this category were the formidable Roman statesman/general Julius Caesar, who extended Rome's power into Gaul (what is now France); Caesar's lover and ally, the notorious Egyptian queen Cleopatra, who challenged the strongest male rulers of her day; and England's stalwart Queen Elizabeth I, whose defeat of the mighty Spanish Armada saved England from subjugation.

Some of history's other movers and shakers were scientists or other thinkers whose ideas and discoveries altered the way people conduct their everyday lives or view themselves and their place in nature. The electric light and other remarkable inventions of Thomas Edison, for example, revolutionized almost every aspect of home-life and the workplace; and the theories of naturalist Charles Darwin lit the way for biologists and other scientists in their ongoing efforts to understand the origins of living things, including human beings.

Still other people who made history were religious leaders and social reformers. The struggles of the Arabic prophet Muhammad more than a thousand years ago led to the establishment of one of the world's great religions—Islam; and the efforts and personal sacrifices of an American reverend named Martin Luther King Jr. brought about major improvements in race relations and the justice system in the United States.

Each anthology in the People Who Made History series begins with an introductory essay that provides a general overview of the individual's life, times, and contributions. The group of essays that follow are chosen for their accessibility to a young adult audience and carefully edited in consideration of the reading and comprehension levels of that audience. Some of the essays are by noted historians, professors, and other experts. Others are excerpts from contemporary writings by or about the pivotal individual in question. To aid the reader in choosing the material of immediate interest or need, an annotated table of contents summarizes the article's main themes and insights.

Each volume also contains extensive research tools, including a collection of excerpts from primary source documents pertaining to the individual under discussion. The volumes are rounded out with an extensive bibliography and a comprehensive index.

Plutarch, the renowned first-century Greek biographer and moralist, crystallized the idea behind Greenhaven's People Who Made History when he said, "To be ignorant of the lives of the most celebrated men of past ages is to continue in a state of childhood all our days." Indeed, since it is people who make history, every modern nation, organization, institution, invention, artifact, and idea is the result of the diligent efforts of one or more individuals, living or dead; and it is therefore impossible to understand how the world we live in came to be without examining the contributions of these individuals.

# Introduction: Adolf Hitler and His Legacy of Destruction

Adolf Hitler: The name is instantly recognizable across the globe. During his lifetime he was adored by thousands, and feared by millions. After his death, when the enormity of his crimes against humanity was revealed, he came to be seen as evil personified. Perhaps no other person in the twentieth century has had such a profound and lasting impact on the world.

Despite his worldwide infamy, however, many of the facts concerning Hitler's life remain unknown. This obscurity is due in part to Hitler's own penchant for secrecy. Although he spent the second half of his life in the public eye, Hitler took great pains to hide his past. He lied in his autobiography, shut down newspapers that dared to write stories about his family, and ordered the destruction of documents concerning his early years. He even went so far as to obliterate Döllersheim, the Austrian village where his father was baptized. Accounts written by people who personally knew Hitler are often problematic, filled with half-truths, spurious gossip, and faulty memories. Those published during Hitler's dictatorship tend to depict him either as a savior or a madman (depending on whether the author was in or out of Hitler's favor), while the memoirs written after the Second World War—especially those by Nazi leaders who were facing execution for wartime atrocities—are crammed with unverifiable "facts" that place the blame for the authors' crimes on Hitler. The primary sources that record Hitler's life contain an unprecedented number of contradictions and unexplainable gaps for such a public persona. According to historian Ian Kershaw, "For all the surviving mountains of paper spewed out by the governmental apparatus of the Third Reich, the sources for reconstructing the life of the German Dictator are in many respects extraordinarily limited."

Yet the secrecy surrounding Hitler's background did not begin with him. It was, in a sense, a family legacy that began with his father, Alois.

## THE FAMILY SECRET

Alois was born illegitimate to a peasant woman named Maria Anna Schicklgruber. The space for his father's name on the baptismal certificate was left blank, and to this day, the identity of his father is still a mystery. For almost forty years, Alois bore his mother's last name.

When Alois Schicklgruber was five years old, his mother married Johann Georg Hiedler, and soon thereafter Alois was sent to live with his stepfather's brother, Johann Nepomuk Hiedler. Both of these men have been suggested as candidates for Alois's biological father, but there is no definitive proof for or against these theories. However, Alois did eventually adopt their last name. At the age of thirty-nine, he returned to the church in Döllersheim where he had been baptized and convinced the local priest that the long-deceased Georg Hiedler had indeed been his biological father. The priest then drew up documentation to officially legitimize Alois; he wrote down Alois's last name as Hitler, which at the time was one of several interchangeable spellings of the name.

There is yet another theory about Alois's father: that he was a Jew, a member of a well-to-do family in whose home Alois's mother worked as a maid. Again, there is no definitive proof, and historians even disagree over whether Maria Schicklgruber ever worked for a Jewish family. But there are indications that a version of this story, true or not, was already circulating during Alois's childhood and continued to surface throughout Adolf Hitler's political career. The rumor that Adolf Hitler's grandfather was Jewish (which would make Adolf one-quarter Jewish) had potential to do him great harm professionally because a large part of his political message was based on violently anti-Semitic ideology. Although the question of Alois's parentage may never be solved, it does seem clear that Adolf Hitler believed he needed to hide the truth about his father's illegitimacy: In 1939, Hitler ordered Döllersheim to be evacuated and turned into an artillery range, presumably in order to ensure the destruction of the records of Alois's baptism and legitimization.

Alois's decision to reverse his illegitimate status was indicative of his personality, for he was very much a self-made man. Born fatherless into rural poverty, Alois left home at a young age and through sheer determination worked his way up to the middle class, becoming an official in the Austrian customs service. By all accounts he was a hardworking and respected man, but he was also a stickler for rules; many of his colleagues and neighbors found him to be stern, pedantic, and humorless. The strict customs official had a wilder side, however. Alois was a flagrant womanizer, fathering illegitimate children of his own. He drank regularly, and he had an explosive, unpredictable temper. All and all, he was not an easy man to live with.

In 1885, Alois married Klara Pölzl. It was by no means a marriage of equals: Alois was forty-seven, while his bride was only twenty-four and had been working in his household as a maid. Alois had already been married twice and had two small children, Alois Jr. and Angela, who had been left motherless when his second wife died. Klara and Alois may also have been related by blood. Klara was the granddaughter of Johann Nepomuk Hiedler, and since Alois had claimed Nepomuk's brother as his father, Klara and Alois were officially considered to be second cousins and had to obtain a papal dispensation before they could be married. If Nepomuk Hiedler was in fact Alois's biological father, then Klara and Alois may have been even more closely related. Long into their marriage, Klara called her husband "Uncle."

Klara took over the care of her stepchildren and had two children of her own in rapid succession. A loving and devoted mother, Klara centered her life around her children. But in the third year of her marriage, tragedy struck: Klara bore a third child who lived only a few days, and shortly thereafter, her other two children contracted diphtheria and died. This terrible loss devastated Klara, and when she became pregnant again several months later, she was apprehensive lest another tragedy occur.

### YOUNG ADOLF

On April 20, 1889, Klara bore her fourth child, Adolf, in the Austrian town of Braunnau am Inn, near the German border. Klara was convinced that her new baby was sickly. Afraid that he might die, she was anxiously overprotective and showered him with affection, blatantly favoring him over her stepchildren. For the first five years of Adolf's life, he was Klara's only child and the center of her attention. Even after his younger siblings, Edmund and Paula, were born, he remained the apple of his mother's eye.

During Adolf's early childhood, his family resided in various locales on the Austrian-German border. Between the ages of three and five, Adolf actually lived on the German side of the border in the city of Passau, which is in the southern region of Bavaria. He played with German children and acquired a Bavarian accent that remained with him throughout his life. The stay in Passau left an indelible impression on the young child, and he would later say that he had always felt himself to be more German than Austrian.

In 1895, the family returned to Austria, and Adolf began school. At first he was a good student, receiving excellent grades. But family tensions intensified that summer, when Alois Hitler retired from the customs service. Now that Alois was home more often, the children increasingly fell under his strict scrutiny. He was a domineering father who expected his children to obey him without question. Whether he also physically abused his children is still a matter of debate among historians. As an adult, Adolf claimed that his father had severely beaten him, but some biographers believe that Adolf created this story just as he fabricated many other elements of his life. On the other hand, Adolf's half-brother Alois Jr. and his sister Paula both corroborated Adolf's story: Alois Jr. described brutal beatings that he and Adolf received from their father, while Paula recalled a period of time when her father gave Adolf a "sound thrashing every day." Life at home became so miserable that Alois Jr. ran away at the age of fourteen.

In 1900, two events occurred that brought eleven-year-old Adolf in direct conflict with his father. First, Adolf's younger brother Edmund died of the measles, leaving Adolf the only son in the house and the focal point of his father's ambitions. Then in the fall, Adolf entered secondary school, and his father insisted that he prepare for a career as a civil servant. But Adolf had no desire to follow in his father's footsteps; instead, he dreamed of becoming an artist. His grades began to plummet—later he claimed that he purposely failed his classes in order to thwart his father's plans for his future career. The battle between Adolf and his father continued until January 1903, when Alois suddenly collapsed and died in a local tavern.

After his father's death, Adolf Hitler remained in school for a while, but he disliked it and eventually convinced his mother to let him drop out at the age of sixteen. His father's pension supplied the family with sufficient funds, so Hitler felt no pressing need to find work. Instead, he spent his days drawing, painting, and reading, while in the evening he often attended the theater or opera. This pleasant life continued undisturbed until 1907, when Hitler decided to travel to Vienna, the capital city of Austria, to take the entrance examinations for the General Painting School of the Vienna Academy of Fine Arts. He passed the first part of the test, but failed the second. Hitler had confidently expected to pass the exams with flying colors, and his failure came as a shock. A second blow followed that December, when his beloved mother died of breast cancer. Klara's doctor later wrote that in all his career, he "never saw anyone so prostrate with grief as Adolf Hitler."

In 1908, Hitler returned to Vienna, where he lived with a friend who was studying at the Academy of Music. Hitler had not told his family about his failure to gain acceptance to the art academy, and for some time he also hid this fact from his roommate. He made some efforts to improve his artistic skills, with an eye toward retaking the entrance examination for the art academy in the fall. This time, he did not even make the first cut.

This second rejection seems to have broken something in Hitler. Shortly afterwards, he cut all ties to his past. While his roommate was out of town, Hitler simply gathered his belongings and left, leaving no word as to where he was going or why. Neither did he attempt to contact his family. At first, he rented a room in Vienna, but within a few months he was living on the streets. In his autobiography, Hitler claimed that he had run out of money, which caused him to sink into "a world of misery and poverty." However, some of Hitler's biographers maintain that his inheritance from his parents and the orphan's pension he received from the state should have provided him with enough money to keep a roof over his head. Instead, they suggest that, deeply depressed by his mother's death and his rejection by the academy, Hitler suffered a nervous breakdown.

### THE FORMATIVE YEARS

Hitler hit rock bottom toward the end of 1909. Wearing little more than rags, he slept in parks or at a shelter for the homeless; during the day, he worked odd jobs or begged.

Some of the other homeless men felt sorry for him, and with their advice and help, Hitler was soon able to better his circumstances. In February 1910, he moved into a men's home that provided more security and comforts than the homeless shelter. Here Hitler began to paint again, selling posters, postcards, and illustrations. For the next few years, he continued to reside in the men's home and to support himself with the modest income he made from his artwork.

According to Hitler, it was during this time period that he adopted his anti-Semitic views. Until his stay in Vienna, he maintained, he had never held any animosity toward Jews and at first was alienated by the anti-Semitism he encountered in Vienna. However, he eventually became an avid reader of the anti-Semitic pamphlets and newspapers that filled the Viennese newsstands. Whether Hitler was entirely truthful about this matter has been debated by historians. On one hand, Hitler probably was exposed to anti-Semitic beliefs well before he came to Vienna: At least one of the teachers at his secondary school was a vocal anti-Semite, and anti-Jewish papers were widely available in his hometown. On the other hand, the evidence suggests that Hitler did not become a hardened anti-Semite in Vienna. Two of his closest associates at the men's home were Jewish, and he conducted most of his business with three Jewish art dealers for whom, according to historian John Toland, "he expressed great regard." Perhaps Hitler's conversion to rabid and unyielding anti-Semitism was more gradual than he admitted. Nevertheless, he was definitely affected by what Kershaw describes as the "poisonous antisemitic atmosphere of the Vienna he knew—one of the most virulently anti-Jewish cities in Europe."

After drifting aimlessly in Vienna for several years, Hitler decided to relocate to Munich, the capital of the Bavarian region of Germany. Here he hoped to continue his art career and possibly establish himself as an architect. Hitler wrote in his autobiography that he left Vienna in 1912, but the historical records show that he actually departed in mid-1913, primarily to evade being drafted into the Austrian army. Presumably he altered the date by a year in order to hide his attempt at dodging the draft. At any rate, his attempt failed: The Austrian police caught up with him in Munich in January 1914. Biographer Joachim Fest writes, "The charge he faced was serious, and Hitler . . . was in imminent danger of a prison sentence." Luck was with him, however; the Austrian draft board ruled that he was "too weak" to bear arms. He was allowed to return to Munich and his life as a small-time artist.

When World War I broke out later that year, though, Hitler eagerly enlisted in the German army. During the next four years, he fought in almost fifty battles and served as a message carrier, which was a very dangerous job. But Hitler seemed to thrive on danger and soon gained a reputation as an extraordinarily courageous soldier. According to author Charles Bracelen Flood, "While the other runners were discussing whose turn it was to take a message forward to a command post under fire, Hitler would put the message into the pouch on his belt and be gone." He was decorated several times for bravery, including the Iron Cross first class, which was rarely given to enlisted men. Hitler loved soldiering, and he later referred to these years as "the greatest and most unforgettable time of my earthly existence." Kershaw explains that "for the first time in his life [Hitler had] a cause, a commitment, comradeship, an external discipline, a sort of regular employment, a sense of well-being, and— more than that—a sense of belonging."

On the night of October 13, 1918, Hitler's unit was caught in a gas attack. Temporarily blinded by the poisonous gas, Hitler was sent to a military hospital for treatment. While there, he learned the shattering news that Germany had been defeated. He could barely comprehend the news; throughout the war, he had believed with a fierce faith that Germany could not lose. When he was released from the hospital, Hitler returned to Munich to find the city in a state of turmoil and revolution. The military put him to work in the propaganda section, lecturing German soldiers returning from the war. He was also assigned to attend political meetings of various fringe groups as an informant. It was in this capacity that he first attended a meeting of a small political group known as the German Workers' Party.

## THE BIRTH OF A POLITICAL CAREER

Initially, Hitler was not greatly impressed with the German Workers' Party, but as he attended more meetings, joined in discussions, and read the party's literature, he changed his mind. Later he claimed to have been the seventh card-carrying member of the party, but in actuality his card indicated that he was the fifty-fifth. It is accurate, however, that he joined the party in its early days and was instrumental in shaping the tiny organization into a powerful political force.

As a lecturer for the German army, Hitler had already started to realize his considerable skills as a public speaker. Now he put his talent to use for the German Workers' Party, and his fiery speeches drew increasingly larger crowds to the party's meetings. By the February 1920 meeting where Hitler presented the party's twenty-five-point political platform, he was able to attract a crowd of nearly two thousand people. Hitler also worked hard to gain entrance to the inner circle of the party. In March 1920, he resigned from the German army in order to concentrate all his time and energy on his political endeavors. At the age of thirty, he had finally discovered his calling in life.

As he gained influence and prestige in the German Workers' Party, he began to shape it more to his liking. In 1920, at Hitler's instigation, the party changed its name to the National Socialist German Workers' Party. (The abbreviation "Nazi" is derived from the German words for National Socialist.) A year later, Hitler threatened to resign from the Nazi Party unless he was made party chairman, with unlimited powers and authority. His demands were granted, and he adopted the title of Führer (leader). He also cultivated the loyalty of the Nazis' paramilitary group known as the Sturmabteilung (SA), or storm troopers.

During this period, Hitler continued to give frequent speeches and also published articles on a regular basis. Here he presented his message to the German people. Hitler argued that the Weimar government, a liberal democratic regime that had been established after World War I, was weak and corrupt. He blamed the government, communists, and Jews for the economic hardships that the Germans had experienced since the war's end. In fact, he maintained, Germany would have won the war had it not been for a traitorous conspiracy between the Jews and the communists. However, Hitler continued, he had faith in the German people's ability to overcome their oppressors; he called on them to ignite a new movement of national pride and might.

Much of Hitler's rhetoric was based on *völkisch* ideology. The German word *völkisch* and the English word "folk" both derive from the same root, but the German term also contains the meaning of an intense nationalism based on racial or ethnic origin. The "central strands" of this concept, according to Kershaw, are "extreme nationalism, racial anti-semitism, and mystical notions of a uniquely German social order, with roots in the Teutonic past, resting on order, harmony, and hierarchy." *Völkisch* ideology did not originate with either Hitler or the Nazi Party; as scholar Joseph Nyomarkay notes, "After 1918, the völkisch concept became a slogan of numerous political forces in Germany and provided a broad umbrella for the diverse right-wing groups fighting against the established political systems." However, Hitler and the Nazis skillfully employed this ideology, arguing that the German Volk were racially superior to the French, the Czechs, the Poles, the Russians—and most of all, the Jews.

In November 1923, Hitler decided the time had come for the Nazis to take over the country. He planned to first gain control of the local Bavarian government and then overthrow the Weimar government in Berlin. On the night of November 8, most of the political leaders of Bavaria attended a meeting in a Munich beer hall. Hitler ordered his SA troops to surround the building; then he burst into the hall, fired a pistol in the air, and shouted that the national revolution had begun. While other SA units forcibly occupied Munich's army headquarters and barracks, Hitler attempted to persuade the leaders of the Bavarian government to support the Nazi cause. The following day, the Nazis organized a march through Munich, but the procession was fired on by the police. Several party members were killed, and Hitler dislocated his shoulder in the melee. He managed to escape but was arrested and imprisoned two days later.

After the failed coup, the situation looked bleak. The German government banned the Nazi Party, and many of the party's top leaders were either in hiding or in jail with Hitler. But Hitler turned the tables at his treason trial, making it a forum for the Nazis. He spoke eloquently and with passion about his vision for Germany, and he gained attention from the international press. He did not deny the charges; rather, he attempted to justify his actions against the government, proclaiming: "I consider myself not a traitor but a German, who desired what was best for his people."

Hitler received a sentence of five years in prison, but he was paroled after only nine months, a relatively light punishment for high treason. During his imprisonment, he began writing a book entitled *Mein Kampf* ("My Struggle"). Half autobiography, half ideological tract, *Mein Kampf* is a poorly written and ponderous book that even many devoted Nazis found impossible to read. The initial sales numbers were far below what Hitler had hoped for. (Once he was in power, the book sold in the millions, but how many Germans actually read it is unknown.) Nevertheless, *Mein Kampf* is an important text. In it, Hitler revealed his intent to set up a dictatorial government, laid out his plans for the conquest of Europe, and vented his intense hatred of the Jews. Unfortunately, only a few of the foreigners who read *Mein Kampf* when it was first published believed that Hitler would follow through with his threats. As William L. Shirer points out in *The Rise and Fall of the Third Reich*, "Had the foreign statesmen of the world perused [*Mein Kampf*] carefully while there was still time, both Germany and the world might have been saved from catastrophe. For whatever other accusations can be made against Adolf Hitler, no one can accuse him of not putting down in writing exactly the kind . . . of world he meant to create."

## HITLER'S RISE TO POWER

Following his release from prison, Hitler immediately started working to rebuild the Nazi Party. This would be a formidable task: After the failed coup, the party had been dissolved, and Hitler had been prohibited from speaking publicly. Nevertheless, he had emerged from prison with a new determination to succeed, this time by working within the political system. He convinced the government to lift the ban on the Nazi Party and then rebuilt it from the grassroots level. In 1928, the party campaigned for the first time in the national elections for the German Reichstag (parliament). The Nazis made a poor showing, winning only twelve seats. The next year, however, the American stock market crashed, sparking a worldwide depression. As the German economy faltered and unemployment ran rampant, the membership of the Nazi Party soared. In the 1930 Reichstag elections, the Nazis captured 107 seats.

For a few weeks in 1931, a scandal involving Hitler's personal life almost derailed the progress of his career. After Hitler's release from prison, his widowed half-sister, Angela Raubal, had moved in with him as his housekeeper. She was accompanied by her seventeen-year-old daughter, Geli. Before long, Hitler became preoccupied with Geli, appearing with her frequently at public venues and allowing her to play the role of hostess at his home. Rumors arose that Hitler was infatuated with his young niece, in love, perhaps even sexually involved. The exact nature of their relationship may never be known, but Hitler seems to have been deeply emotionally attached to her. Then, in 1931, Geli was found in Hitler's flat, shot dead with his gun. The anti-Nazi press had a field day with the story, insinuating that Hitler had killed Geli in a rage of jealous passion. But Hitler had an alibi; he was not in town when the shooting occurred. Geli's death was ruled a suicide. Nonetheless, historians still debate whether Geli took her own life, and if so, whether some sordid or violent aspect of her relationship with Hitler led her to resort to such a desperate act.

Whatever role Hitler may have had in Geli's death, it tore him apart as nothing had since his mother's death years before. He sank into a deep depression and went into seclusion for two weeks, under constant suicide watch by his fellow Nazis. Eventually he regained his composure and threw himself back into his work. But Hitler never forgot Geli; he carried her photo with him for the rest of his life and observed her birth and death dates religiously.

Once the threat of scandal had passed, Hitler concentrated on increasing his political power. Although the Nazis had made impressive gains in the Reichstag, as an Austrian citizen Hitler had been unable to serve in the German government. In early 1932, he rectified this situation by becoming a German citizen. Then he entered the presidential campaign against the incumbent, Paul von Hindenburg, an aging and widely respected World War I commander. Although Hitler lost the election, he garnered a considerable percentage of the vote, boosting his political prestige. In the Reichstag elections that were held shortly thereafter, the Nazis won 230 seats, making Hitler the leader of the most powerful political party in Germany. He decided to use this new status to demand that Hindenburg appoint him as chancellor, a position similar to prime minister. Initially Hindenburg refused; he said the Nazis were too violent, too intolerant, too anti-Jewish. But the Nazi Reichstag members and many prominent German businessmen put such pressure on Hindenburg that he finally acceded. On January 30, 1933, Hitler was sworn in as chancellor of Germany.

## BUILDING A DICTATORSHIP

Hindenburg was right to be wary of Hitler's intentions, for Hitler immediately took steps to consolidate his power and crush any opposition to the Nazi Party. First he called for new Reichstag elections. During the election campaign, the Nazis resorted to violence and intimidation against their political opponents. As historian Alan Bullock writes, "Although the other parties were still allowed to function, their meetings were broken up, their speakers assaulted and beaten, their posters torn down and their papers continually suppressed." On February 27, the Reichstag building was destroyed by arson, and the Nazis swiftly placed the blame on their chief political rivals, the communists. Who really set the fire is still uncertain: Some historians believe that the Nazis secretly torched the building on Hitler's orders, while others argue that a lone communist agitator—acting without party leaders' knowledge—was responsible. Regardless of the fire's true origin, Hitler eagerly exploited the disaster, rounding up thousands of communists and convincing Hindenburg to issue emergency decrees suspending free speech and free press. These measures helped the Nazi Party to win 44 percent of the vote in the Reichstag elections.

On March 23, the Reichstag passed the Enabling Act, which conferred dictatorial powers on Hitler. Under the Enabling Act, he could enact laws and even suspend the constitution without the approval of the Reichstag. The passage of this act sounded the death knell for the Weimar Republic and allowed Hitler to begin creating his Third Reich, the German empire that he predicted would last a thousand years. There was no room in Hitler's Third Reich for political opposition, so one of his first steps was to ban all parties besides the Nazis. He moved against any entity that might jeopardize his power: The state governments of Germany were consolidated under national Nazi control, labor unions were abolished, and newspapers were shut down. In June 1934, Hitler even purged his own party, ordering the execution of those members whom he considered to be enemies or potential threats.

At the same time, Hitler sought to win over the hearts and minds of the German people. With the German economy still in shambles, one of Hitler's first priorities was to decrease unemployment by instituting an enormous public works program. He also established state-sponsored organizations for different sections of society, such as farmers, teachers, and veterans. The most successful of these organizations was the Hitler Youth, which indoctrinated children between the ages of ten and eighteen in Nazi ideology. Further indoctrination took place through a massive propaganda campaign that promoted Hitler and the Nazis as the saviors of Germany. As Bullock explains, "Hitler . . . told the German people to hold up their heads and rediscover their old pride and self-confidence. Germany, united and strong, would end the crippling divisions which had held her back, and recover the place that was her due in the world. Many people believed this in 1933 and thought that a new era had begun."

A new era had indeed begun for some of Germany's citizens, but the future that Hitler had in mind for them was not so rosy. Hitler's hatred for Jewish people had continued to grow over the years, and the Nazi Party was itself intensely anti-Semitic. As soon as Hitler came to power, he instituted laws that discriminated against Jews. For example, the number of Jewish students who were allowed to attend schools and universities was sharply limited, while Jewish professors, government workers, and physicians were forced to retire. Hitler held national boycotts of Jewish-owned businesses and book burnings of "non-German" literature. Much of Nazi propaganda was slanted against Jews, blaming them for Germany's economic and social woes. The more the Nazis scapegoated the Jews, the more anti-Semitic violence increased, and injured Jews discovered to their dismay that the police and the courts sided with their attackers. Faced with such intense discrimination and terrorization, those Jews who were able to leave fled Germany for other parts of Europe.

## THE FÜHRER

After the passage of the Enabling Act, Hitler became for all intents and purposes the dictator of Germany. Hindenburg, however, was still president, although his role had been reduced to that of a figurehead. Hitler did not dare to demand complete obedience from the German people while the popular and respected president held office. But Hindenburg was old and in bad health, and Hitler knew he simply needed to bide his time. Hours after Hindenburg died on August 2, 1934, Hitler announced that he was merging the offices of chancellor and president, making himself the sole

*Adolf Hitler at the height of his power*

head of state and the commander-in-chief of the armed forces. Henceforth he was to be addressed as the Führer.

With his control over Germany now unimpeded, Hitler focused on achieving his two main goals: the elimination of the Jews and the physical expansion of his Third Reich. In 1935, he took the first small steps toward achieving both ends. On September 15, the Nazi-controlled Reichstag passed the Nuremberg Laws, which introduced even more severe restrictions for German Jews. Under the laws, Jews were deprived of German citizenship; in addition, they were forbidden to marry non-Jewish Germans or employ non-Jewish maids in their households. According to Kershaw, the Nuremberg Laws "provided the framework for the mass of subsidiary decrees that in the following years were to push German Jews to the outer fringes of society, prisoners in their own land."

Hitler also announced a massive military rearmament in 1935, even though this ran counter to the terms Germany had agreed to in the Treaty of Versailles after the First World War. Hitler revived the general draft, revealed the existence of a German air force, and ordered the rapid expansion of the German army and navy. The following year, he established the Four-Year Plan, a program intended to prepare the German economy for large-scale warfare. In 1936 and 1937, Hitler formed military alliances with Japan and Italy in anticipation of a war.

Despite Hitler's remilitarization of Germany, the nation's territorial expansion initially involved little fighting. Hitler's first move was to retake the Rhineland, an industrially important strip of southwestern Germany that bordered France. After World War I, the Rhineland had been occupied by the French as a demilitarized buffer zone between France and Germany. In March 1936, against the advice of his generals, Hitler ordered his troops to march into the Rhineland. Had the French attacked, the smaller German army would have been forced to retreat. However, though the French protested, they made no move against the German soldiers.

Next Hitler set his sights on his homeland of Austria. The majority of Austria's population was ethnically German, and Hitler had long spoken of his desire for an Anschluss (reunification) of the two countries. In March 1938, the German army marched on Austria, but the soldiers never had to fire a shot. Through a combination of intimidation and diplomatic maneuvers, Hitler secured the resignation of the top Austrian officials; he then proclaimed Austria "a province of the German Reich." On March 14, Hitler made a triumphant entry into Vienna, welcomed by cheering crowds. He who had once wandered Vienna's streets as a hungry and homeless outcast now returned as a conquering hero. "When Hitler entered Vienna," Fest remarks, "amid cheering and the tolling of bells, he was enjoying the realization of his earliest dream. The [city] that had witnessed his failures, had disdained and humiliated him, at last lay at his feet in admiration, shame, and fear."

Hitler's final bloodless victory was Czechoslovakia. First he undertook the annexation of the Sudetenland, an area of Czechoslovakia that bordered southeastern Germany and was largely populated by ethnic Germans. The Czechs, Hitler claimed, were grossly mistreating the ethnic Germans of the Sudetenland, and he threatened to retaliate by attacking Czechoslovakia. Anxious to avoid a war, Britain and France pressured the Czech government to placate Hitler by giving Germany the Sudetenland in the autumn of 1938. As in Austria, many of the ethnic Germans in the Sudetenland welcomed Hitler as a liberator. But Hitler was not satisfied with this small strip of land; in March 1939, he sent his troops into the rest of Czechoslovakia. Once more, the combination of Germany's show of force and Hitler's use of extreme intimidation tactics with the Czech leaders allowed him to capture the country without firing a shot.

Hitler now focused on Poland. He demanded the return of an area of land called the Polish Corridor, which had belonged to Germany prior to the First World War. When Poland's leaders refused, Hitler was infuriated and began to plan his attack. He determined that he would need the help of the Soviet Union in conquering Poland. Hitler's opinion of the Soviets was similar to his feelings about Jews; he had never made a secret of his hatred of communists and Russians. Now, however, he approached Soviet dictator Joseph Stalin with a deal: If the Soviet Union did not come to Poland's aid against a German invasion, Hitler would divide the Polish lands between them. Only days after Stalin had agreed to this arrangement, Germany invaded Poland.

## WORLD WAR II

One of the primary reasons that Hitler had been able to gain so much territory with so little effort was that the leaders of Great Britain, France, and the other Allied nations of the First World War had allowed him to do so. Desperate to avoid a repetition of the terrible destruction and loss of human life in World War I, the leaders of Great Britain and France gave into Hitler's demands rather than declaring war against Germany. However, the invasion of Poland was the last straw.

The leaders of Great Britain and France no longer believed that Hitler was only interested in regaining lands that had formerly belonged to Germany, and they could no longer stand by while Hitler carved up Europe to his liking. On September 3, two days after the German invasion of Poland, France and Great Britain declared war on Germany. The Second World War had begun.

However, this declaration of war came too late to save Poland: Within three weeks, the Germans had devastated the much smaller and ill-equipped Polish army. While France and Great Britain were still mobilizing their forces, Hitler's army overran Norway, Denmark, Belgium, Holland, and Luxembourg in swift succession. When France fell in June 1940, Hitler was ecstatic. He insisted that the French leaders sign the armistice at the exact same spot where Germany had surrendered to France in the First World War.

Hitler had come a long way since his days as an itinerant artist. He now commanded a sizable portion of Europe, and there seemed to be no end to his military successes. He lived in luxurious surroundings and was accompanied everywhere by fawning admirers. Yet in many respects, he continued to live the unconventional life of an artist. Typically he slept late and then lingered over his breakfast and morning newspapers, often not emerging from his private quarters until well after noon. He frequently spent two to three hours over lunch with his colleagues, discussing his grandiose architectural plans for Berlin or Munich. In the evening, his inner circle—including his longtime mistress, Eva Braun—would meet to watch movies or listen to Hitler reminisce about the Nazis' early years. Hitler could—and usually did—go on until two or three in the morning, when his guests had to fight to stifle their yawns.

Hitler's comfortable life stands in stark contrast to the misery that he and the Nazis were at the very same time inflicting on Europe's Jews. Hitler had continued to ratchet up the restrictions against the Jews, ordering them to wear yellow stars and forcibly removing them into ghettos, where wretched conditions ensured that thousands died of starvation or disease. Toward the end of 1941, the Nazis opened the first of the death camps, designed specifically as a "final solution" to "the Jewish problem." Before the fall of Nazi Germany, an estimated 6 million Jews were murdered in these camps, as well as approximately 5 million more people—gypsies, political dissidents, intellectuals, homo-sexuals, and others whom Hitler considered undesirable.

## HITLER'S MISTAKES

Hitler's stunning military successes were even more spec-tacular in light of the fact that he undertook most of them against the better judgment of his military advisers. From 1936 to 1940, Hitler's generals repeatedly warned him that his plans for conquest would fail disastrously, and Hitler re-peatedly proved them wrong. He came to believe that his de-cisions, made on instinct, were far superior to his generals' formal military training and years of experience. However, Hitler's instinct began to fail him in 1941. On June 22, ig-noring his advisers' reservations, Hitler doublecrossed Stalin by invading the Soviet Union. The invasion at first ap-peared to be another success for Germany, and Hitler over-confidently declared in October that Russia "is already beaten and will never rise again." If the German army had in fact conquered the Soviet Union by October, Hitler's inva-sion might have succeeded. But although the German army had made considerable advances, the Russians had not yet surrendered. The German troops were completely unpre-pared for the onset of the severe Russian winter, and by De-cember the Soviets began to counterattack.

The Germans regained some ground during the spring and summer of 1942, but once again the Soviets ruled the winter. In November, the Russians trapped the German Sixth Army at Stalingrad. Hitler's generals advised him that there was only one recourse: Let the Sixth Army try to break through the Russian line and retreat. Hitler refused. He insisted that the Sixth Army hold its ground and capture Stalingrad. Nor would he listen to any talk of surrender. According to historian Fred Weinstein, Hitler believed "if they were truly overwhelmed then they should fight to the death, as instinct dictated." This belief cost Hitler thousands of soldiers at Stalingrad. When the last remnants of the Sixth Army did surrender in early 1943, Hitler was enraged by what he saw as their cowardice. From this point on, the Soviets took the offensive against the Ger-mans, steadily pushing them out of Russia.

Besides invading Russia, Hitler made another enormous mistake in 1941: He declared war on the United States. When Japan bombed American ships at Pearl Harbor in Hawaii in December 1941, the United States immediately de-

clared war on Japan. Because Japan and Germany were allies, Hitler declared war on the United States. In doing so,
notes historian Eugene Davidson, "Hitler added a fresh,
now-open enemy with incalculable resources to his list. . . .
The new enemy was as yet only a cloud on the horizon,
though it would grow rapidly." By 1943, American bombers
were pounding German cities in extensive air raids. On June
6, 1944, American, British, and other Allied troops landed on
the Normandy coast of France, opening a second front in the
European war. As the Allies pushed westward through
France toward Germany, the Russians launched a brutal assault against the German front in the East. The tide of the
war had turned irrevocably against the Nazis.

## THE FALL OF HITLER'S REICH

The strain of the war, and especially the stress of the mounting defeats, took a heavy toll on Hitler's physical health. He
was only in his 50s, but between 1941 and 1944, he appeared
to age tremendously. Plagued by stomach cramps, head-
aches, and insomnia, he increasingly relied on injections of
amphetamines. Many historians believe that Hitler became
addicted to drugs. Furthermore, his trusted personal physi-
cian was apparently a quack; he overmedicated Hitler and
prescribed poisonous substances such as strychnine and
belladonna. "During the course of 1943," Bullock states,
"Hitler began to suffer from a trembling of his left arm and
left leg, which . . . steadily became more pronounced and refused to yield to any treatment. . . . At the same time he began
to drag his left foot, as though he were lame." He was also
growing more paranoid and disoriented, flying into hysterical fits when his generals dared to question his orders.
Shortly after the Allied invasion of Normandy, a group of
German military officers attempted to assassinate Hitler
with a time bomb. Although Hitler walked away from the
blast, he sustained several injuries, and his tremors grew
even more uncontrollable.

By the beginning of 1945, the end was near for both Hitler
and his vaunted thousand-year Reich. Soviet troops crossed
into Germany, heading for Berlin from the east, while American and British forces swept toward Berlin from the west.
Hitler holed up in his underground concrete bunker in
Berlin, where, as biographer Robert Payne describes, he
"still went through the motions of waging war. Enfeebled,

prematurely old, his mind broken under the strain, he continued to receive his generals and give orders that would never be obeyed." He urged Eva Braun to flee for safety, but instead she made a dangerous trek through a bomb raid in order to reach the bunker and then refused to leave his side. On April 25, with Berlin surrounded by the Russian army, Hitler finally realized that the war was lost. He dreaded what might happen to him if he were captured and so began planning his own death. Early on the morning of April 29, as artillery shells exploded outside the bunker, he married Eva Braun. The following day, Hitler and his wife said goodbye to the staff and retired to their private quarters. They each bit into a capsule of cyanide, and Hitler then shot himself in the head. Their bodies were hastily cremated in the garden outside the bunker.

A week later, the German army surrendered, bringing to a close one of the most horrific episodes in human history.

## THE ENDURING ENIGMA

Even before Hitler's death, Allied troops had discovered and liberated some of the Nazi death camps. After the war's end, as the full extent of the Holocaust became known, a stunned world asked the questions: Why did Hitler do it? What drove him to order the cold-blooded murder of millions of innocent human beings?

Historians, psychologists, and numerous other scholars have tried to answer these questions. These commentators have suggested a wide range of theories. Many believe that Hitler was mentally ill: Paranoid schizophrenia, manic depression, and borderline personality disorder are among the more frequent diagnoses. Others theorize that Hitler may have suffered from a physical illness that affected his brain, such as advanced syphilis or encephalitis. Some point to his troubled childhood, blaming a violently abusive father and an overprotective, indulgent mother for warping young Adolf's personality. Thousands upon thousands of pages have been written in the attempt to solve this mystery, yet to this day, all the suggested solutions remain unproven theories.

Of all the questions surrounding Adolf Hitler's life, this is the largest, the most important—and the one most likely never to be answered. Even renowned scholars have thrown up their hands in despair. Historian and biographer Alan Bullock has declared, "The more I learn about Adolf Hitler, the harder I find it to explain and accept what followed," while Jewish theologian Emil Fackenheim has concluded that "there will never be an adequate explanation. . . . The closer one gets to explicability the more one realizes nothing can make Hitler explicable." Nevertheless, the study of Hitler's life, career, and crimes is of crucial importance. It is only by grappling with the enigma of Adolf Hitler that humanity can learn what measures might prevent a reoccurrence of the evil he inflicted on the world.

This volume of Greenhaven's People Who Made History series is intended to serve as an introduction to the vast wealth of literature concerning Hitler's life and times. The essays included in this anthology were carefully selected to present an expansive overview of Hitler's life and the essential aspects of his career. In particular, the essays explore Hitler's creation of the two events that irrevocably changed the world: World War II and the Holocaust. Noted historians and scholars discuss the possible influences that led Hitler to choose this path, the responsibility he bears for the tragic results, and the lasting historical significance of his life and deeds. These chapters are supplemented by an appendix of primary source documents that provide examples of Hitler's speeches and writings, as well as enlightening commentaries from those who knew him personally or who lived through his regime. Among the other useful features of this volume are the detailed chronology and a bibliography of primary and secondary sources for further research.

The People Who Made History series is dedicated to the examination of those individuals who, through their ideas and actions, significantly affected the course of human history. The inclusion of Adolf Hitler in this series serves as a bracing reminder: A single person can set the world on a course of unimaginable suffering and destruction, but only if others stand by and do nothing. As Kershaw notes, "Hitler's dictatorship amounted to the collapse of modern civilization—a form of nuclear blow-out within modern society. It showed what we are capable of." This, perhaps, is the most important legacy that Hitler left the world: the sobering realization that humanity is capable of great evil. And the most important lesson to be learned from Hitler's life is the necessity of eternal vigilance to prevent such evil from ever being unleashed again.

## CHAPTER 1

# Hitler's Early Life and Influences

# Hitler's Failure as an Artist

Henry Grosshans

As a youth, Adolf Hitler aspired to an artistic career. He wanted to study at the Academy of Fine Arts in Vienna but failed the entrance exam twice. During the next few years, Hitler remained in Vienna, attempting to make a living as an artist. Even after his rise to political power, Hitler maintained an active interest in art and architecture, but he was violently opposed to modern art, which he considered degenerate. Under Nazi rule, many modern artists were persecuted, and their works banned or destroyed. In the following selection, taken from his book *Hitler and the Artists,* Henry Grosshans describes Hitler's experiences in Vienna and his isolation from the revolutionary changes that were then taking place in the art world. Grosshans examines how Hitler's failure to gain acceptance to the academy or establish himself as a successful artist may have influenced his later attitudes and actions. Grosshans taught history for many years at Washington State University in Pullman.

In September 1907, the eighteen-year-old Adolf Hitler arrived in Vienna to take the examination for entrance into the General School of Painting at the Academy of Fine Arts. He had completed in the provincial Austrian towns of Fischlam, Lambach, Leonding, Linz, and Steyr the only structured education he was to receive—one of his teachers was later to describe him as "distinctly talented, if in a rather narrow sense, but he lacked self-discipline, being generally regarded as obstinate, high-handed, intransigent, and fiery-tempered"—and he had, according to his own testimony, set his heart upon becoming an artist. His father was dead, his mother in Linz was mortally ill, and Hitler was, one could say, on his own.

## HITLER'S TEST RESULTS

The Academy examination was in two parts, and one hundred and thirteen candidates presented themselves. The first part required applicants to perform exercises based upon such subjects as Cain and Abel, the Prodigal Son, Winter, Shipwreck, Joy and Moonlight. Thirty-three of the aspiring artists failed this part of the examination; Hitler, however, was admitted to the second phase, the presentation of "sample drawings," original work that could be evaluated by the examiners. Here Hitler did not meet the standards set, and an entry beside his name read, "Test drawing unsatisfactory." (Of the one hundred and thirteen candidates, only twenty-eight passed both parts of the examination and were admitted to the Academy.) Upon being told that his talents might lie in the field of architecture, Hitler attempted to gain entrance to the Vienna Architectural School. But he did not possess the necessary credentials for such admission. He returned to Linz. His mother died in December, and by the following February, Hitler was again in Vienna, where he took painting lessons and prepared for a second attempt to secure entrance to the Academy. The 1908 examination, however, was a disaster. He failed the first part—the section he had successfully completed in 1907—and the words "Not admitted to the test" beside his name were brutal and definitive.

The effects of this failure upon Hitler are difficult to assess, and we are left largely with suppositions, some valuable and some useless. Hitler was undoubtedly disappointed and perhaps even shamed by this turn of events. He had experienced his first serious defeat at the hands of a professional bureaucracy, and his boyhood dreams of artistic triumph had been reduced to the terrifying phrase, "Not admitted to the test." It is likely that this outcome did stimulate a latent suspicion, even hatred, of authority, and it may be that an artist scorned is an artist enraged. One possessing an artistic temperament, or who sees himself as an artist, may find it impossible to accept the adverse judgments of others or to seek fulfillment in alternative professions or occupations. Certainly there is no evidence that Hitler ever considered returning to Linz or thought of preparing himself for some other career. Rather, he decided to become an independent artist, without benefit of further training and outside the usually recognized artistic circles. He isolated himself from previous acquaintances and set out on his solitary way.

Hitler was to remain in Vienna for the next four and a half years. Many details of his life during this period have been pieced together, although an absence of certain important facts still forces us often to rely upon conjecture and careful consideration of the suspect evidence. It has been well established that those who knew Hitler for brief periods of time in Vienna, or later claimed to have known him, embellished their recollections after Hitler became famous and are, in great part, unreliable authorities. In *Mein Kampf* Hitler devotes many pages to comments upon his Viennese experience, and the book is a valuable source for understanding its author. But the autobiography, written over ten years after Hitler departed Vienna, was basically a polemic addressed to followers disheartened by the failure of the 1923 attempt to overthrow the Bavarian government. Moreover, the volume's wandering repetitions, its rhetorical excesses, and its lack of specific information raise suspicions about its reliability as an authoritative statement of actual circumstances being described. *Mein Kampf* is definitely not a "confession," an attempt to show the ambiguities, the self-doubts, the painful efforts to achieve enlightenment. Rather, it is a series of declarations, an arrogant, self-promoting exercise, a document that had other purposes than to provide an accurate and thoughtful analysis of life in Vienna. Hitler had initially planned to entitle the book *A Reckoning,* and the ultimate subtitle was *Settling Accounts*—an indication of the disputatious nature of the volume. Also, when writing *Mein Kampf,* Hitler undoubtedly ascribed many of his ideas of the early nineteen-twenties to the period when he lived in the Austrian capital, possibly because he did believe that he had arrived at certain conclusions about history and culture at an earlier date, or because the static nature of the autobiography did not stimulate any attempt to show a progression of thought but, rather, encouraged the author to state unquestioned truths that he was convinced he had been aware of during his entire adult life.

## DOWN AND OUT IN VIENNA

In Vienna the young Hitler drifted down into the world of flophouses, cheap meals, and the anonymity of the faceless nondescript, although he did not suffer the extreme economic deprivation that he later claimed. He was to write with excessive self-dramatization: "I, too, have been tossed around by life in the metropolis; in my skin I could feel the effects of this fate and taste them with my soul." He may, as has been suggested by some students of the period, have written poems, short stories, and plays, and perhaps even the libretto for an opera that was to be patterned after Richard Wagner's *Ring*. And he painted numerous small pictures, in oil and watercolor, at times as many as six or seven a week, pictures of the Parliament building, theaters, bridges, and churches. Hitler himself states that by 1909 (he was then twenty years old) he was working independently as a draftsman and a painter of watercolors. His pictures, signed "A. Hitler," "A.H.," "Hitler Adolf," or "Hitler," were sold to dealers and others by Reinhold Hanisch, a fellow down-and-outer, with artist and agent dividing the sums received and thus supporting each other in the struggle for survival. After quarreling with Hanisch in 1910, Hitler sold his pictures through a dealer or directly to clients. He also prepared posters for merchants that served as advertisements for talcum powder, colored candles, and soap.

And he read, attended opera, concert, and theater performances, and thought about what he saw and experienced. *Mein Kampf* is replete with references to the impact of the years spent in Vienna. We read: "In this period there took shape within me a world picture and a philosophy which became the granite foundation of all my acts. In addition to what I then created, I have had to learn little; and I have had to alter nothing." And again:

> Yet Vienna was and remained for me the hardest, though most thorough, school of my life. I had set foot in this town while still a boy and left it a man, grown quiet and grave. In it I attained the foundations for a philosophy in general and a political view in particular which later I only needed to supplement in detail, but which never left me.

The Vienna of the decade preceding the outbreak of World War I has often been described as a place of gracious living, coffee houses, and sweet talk, a golden city of music, high culture, and what Stefan Zweig in *The World of Yesterday* called "epicurean" delights. The presence of the writers Arthur Schnitzler and Hugo von Hofmannsthal, the theatrical director Max Reinhardt, the composers Gustav Mahler and Arnold

Schoenberg, the artists Oskar Kokoschka, Gustav Klimt, and Egon Schiele, the satirist and critic Karl Kraus, the psychologist Sigmund Freud, and the architect Adolf Loos made Vienna a city of intellectual and artistic light, a metropolis of innovative thinkers, of haunting memories, of sentiment and sentimentality, the Paris of central Europe, even a state of mind expressed in both its nostalgia and its bathos in Rudolf Sieczynski's 1913 composition *Vienna, City of My Dreams.*

Hitler did not participate in this high Viennese culture, and he was, in fact, ultimately to become the intellectual and historical opponent of most of those associated with the glories of the city. He remained a "border Austrian," finding refuge in a shelter maintained for the homeless by a philanthropic organization and then in a men's hostel. He experienced the diseased underside of the capital, the iron brutality of squalor that was the often-ignored aspect of the last years of the Habsburg Empire. And, he later argued, he grew to hate the city. Stimulated by his solitude, by his sense of failure, perhaps by an acquaintance with examples of the gutter literature so prevalent in Vienna (in *Mein Kampf* he states that in 1909, "For a few hellers [coins] I bought the first anti-Semitic pamphlets in my life"), and, perhaps again, by some personal quirk of character, Hitler developed a series of grievances that became a permanent part of his historical interpretation.

## ANTI-SEMITISM AND MODERN ART

It is generally accepted that it was in Vienna that Hitler first gave any considered attention to the matter of race, and he was to write that by the end of his stay in Austria, "I had ceased to be a weak-kneed cosmopolitan and had become an anti-Semite." How well developed this anti-Semitism was by 1913, the year he departed Vienna, is difficult to say. He had probably experienced erotic disgust at the thought of sexual relations between Jew and Gentile, had concluded that Marxism was a Jewish conspiracy, and had accepted the idea that Jewish commercial and financial interests played a nefarious role in European politics. But all this was rather run-of-the-mill anti-Semitism, and it is questionable whether he had yet focused his hatreds or had arrived at a consistent historical analysis. The belief that syphilis, which was endemic in Vienna and for which Hitler had a special horror, and prostitution were directly related to the presence of the Jews was a staple of the coarser strains of Viennese anti-Semitism. Hitler also unquestionably dramatized his first encounter with a Jew when he wrote: "Once, as I was strolling through the Inner City, I suddenly encountered an apparition in a black caftan and black hair locks. Is this a Jew? was my first thought." Then Hitler asked himself: "Is this a German?" Similarly, his response to the fact that a number of Viennese Jewish males were at this time marrying Gentile girls was presented in lurid and exaggerated detail: "the black-haired Jewish youth lurks in wait for the unsuspecting girl, whom he defiles with his blood, thus stealing her from her family."

Hitler's hostility toward Vienna and his anti-Semitism contributed to his general cultural interpretation and to his reaction to the new art of the twentieth century. He was to associate modernity with historical decline, and as he saw the Jew as a threat to the racial health of the community, so he looked upon modern art as a menace to the European cultural consciousness. He wrote in *Mein Kampf* that:

> One of the most obvious signs of decay in the old Reich was the slow decline of the cultural level. . . . Even before the turn of the century an element began to intrude into our art which up to that time could be regarded as entirely foreign and unknown. To be sure, even in earlier times there were occasional aberrations of taste, but such cases were rather artistic derailments, to which posterity could attribute at least a certain historical value, than products no longer of an artistic degeneration, but of a spiritual degeneration that had reached the point of destroying the spirit. In them the political collapse, which later became more visible, was culturally indicated.

How many examples of modern art Hitler actually saw in Vienna is uncertain, and he was not specific as to particular painters or paintings. Rather, his condemnation was general and inclusive. Modern art, in his eyes, was a "pestilence," and, as one would expect, such art became another crime committed by the Jews: "The fact that nine-tenths of all literary filth, artistic trash, and theatrical idiocy can be set to the account of a people, constituting hardly one-hundredth of the country's inhabitants, could simply not be talked away; it was the plain truth." That Hitler's facts here, even when allowing for the important part played by Jews in Viennese cultural life, were inaccurate was, of course, of little consequence to him. It was enough that "What had to be reckoned heavily against the Jews in my eyes was when I became acquainted with their activity in the press, art, literature, and the theater."

## REJECTION OF ARTISTIC DEVELOPMENT

But Hitler's response to modern art was much more than an expression of his anti-Semitism, important as that was. From his early twenties, he was dedicated to a heroic, monumental art that would project a clear connection of viewer and object, that would provide unambiguous guidance in the search for the true and the beautiful. He was attracted to painting and sculpture that would challenge the viewer to strive toward some lofty ideal, recapitulate historical experience, relate some tale of glorious achievement, or illustrate the harmony of the individual and the environment. Thus he rejected any meaningful contact with the crucial artistic development that took place in Europe during the first decade and a half of the twentieth century.

In the years from 1900 to 1914 Western art was truly transformed. Meyer Schapiro has put the situation dramatically: "The world of art had never known so keen an appetite for action, a kind of militancy that gave to cultural life the quality of a revolutionary movement or the beginnings of a new religion." And he has also noted the implications of the new painting: "In the twentieth century the ideal of an imageless art of painting was realized for the first time, and the result was shocking—an arbitrary play with forms and colors that had only a vague connection with visible nature." There occurred what Schapiro calls a surge toward "a boundless modernity," and the significant art of the time became identified by its choice of distinctly unheroic, contemporary figures, by its stress upon new interpretations of postures, gestures, and costumes, and by the search for novelty. Never before in European history had artists set out so consciously and so violently to change the physical appearance of their subjects, and by the time Hitler arrived in Vienna what we think of as the European modernist movement was well under way. . . .

Locked in his own thoughts and in his limiting environment, Hitler did not participate in any of this argument over the use of color, the nature of the subject, the new ideas about light and shade, the pressing upon the outer edges of artistic perception. . . . Hitler was no traveler, geographically or intellectually; he corresponded with no fellow artists, and he took no part in any fruitful if interminable discussion about the meaning of artistic creativity. It is unlikely that he read any of the important documents on modern art that appeared while he was in Vienna, and his own art illustrates his failure to participate in the modernist experience. Watercolors such as *Auersperg Palais* and *Karlskirche* are true examples of inferior "postcard" art—dated, stiff, and with little to commend them save the curiosity aroused by our knowledge of their creator. In *Hitler's Youth*, Franz Jetzinger argues that Hitler's Viennese drawings and paintings are not original, but copies, and claims that Hitler did not draw from life. More important, there is no life in the work, and these buildings, parks, and monuments are stale and stilted. One need only compare Hitler's pictures with Karl Schmidt-Rottluff's *Berlin Street* and Ernst Kirchner's *Tramlines in Dresden*, both painted in 1909, or with Emil Nolde's 1910 etchings of Hamburg, with, as has been said, their "noise and uproar, tumult and smoke and life," to see immediately the gulf separating Hitler's approach from that of the modernists. And anything such as Erich Heckel's 1913 *Glassy Day* or Kirchner's *Five Women in the Street* of the same year was absolutely beyond Hitler.

Art critics commonly argue that "deciphering" the paintings of Pablo Picasso and Georges Braque at this time was similar to attempting to understand a foreign language through a few unrelated words. But Hitler's art requires no "deciphering." It suggests no contact with the intellectual and creative adventure that was modern art, and we are not confronted with any problem of moving time or changing spatial relations. Some of the efforts he was to make during World War I—the sketch *Dugout at Fournes*, the watercolor *Haubourdin*, the pen-and-wash drawing of German infantrymen playing draughts in a trench—and the 1913 oil painting *Schliersee* are not too dissimilar to some of the work being undertaken by now-recognized German artists in 1900 and compare well with the attempts of other politician-painters such as Winston Churchill and Dwight Eisenhower. But Hitler was already a dozen years out of date, and he was to remain impervious to that turbulent artistic ferment of the early years of the twentieth century. His perception remained imprisoned in the stiff and monumental formalism that appears in his Viennese paintings and was to be characteristic of his prewar Munich watercolors such as *Alter Hof* and

*Feldherrnhalle.* Whatever may have been Hitler's possibilities as an artist—and some, such as the theatrical producer Gordon Craig and the historian Werner Maser, have seen potential in the early work—he did not capitalize upon them.

Kirchner, Max Beckmann, . . . Franz Marc, August Macke, Heckel, . . . Schmidt-Rottluff—and Hitler—were born in the eighteen-eighties. But they were contemporaries only in a simple, chronological sense. They were to see different realities, respond to different aesthetic imperatives, and pledge their loyalties to different interpretations of the human situation. Beckmann believed that he could only speak with people who already carried within them a similar metaphysical code. And Hitler's metaphysical code, formed by his temperament and his experiences, made impossible any sympathetic response to modern art or modern artists. A friend once wrote that Macke had an insatiable curiosity for life, and Marc admitted that he made the most outrageous demands upon his imagination. But Hitler's road stretched in another direction, ultimately toward the supposed security of the organized human spirit, toward the confining of what was called Paul Klee's "limitless fancy," toward the dream of the master builder wherein racial memories and racial aspirations were to be incorporated into the artistic expression of the frozen model that would, he believed, provide Europe with its aesthetic standard for the next millennium.

## ABANDONING THE ART WORLD

In May 1913 Adolf Hitler left Vienna for Munich. Upon his arrival in the Bavarian city, he registered with the police as a "painter and writer." Bradley F. Smith writes that Hitler at this time was "still chasing the will-o'-the-wisp of an artist's life." But it may be that as he left Vienna Hitler was drifting and realized that he was not going to become a great artist. He continued to paint and to read in Munich, but he wrote in January 1914, "I earn my living as a self-employed artist, but I do so only in order to continue my education, being otherwise quite without means. I can only devote a very small part of my time to earning as I am still learning to be an architectural painter." He was to retain throughout his life an interest in art and was to treasure what he regarded as his unique artistic insights. But historical circumstances were to open new possibilities, and war, social disorder, and historical confusion were to carry him away from the artist's career.

# The Intellectual Roots of Hitler's Anti-Semitism

Robert G.L. Waite

Robert G.L. Waite is a retired professor of history
who taught for forty years at Williams College in
Williamstown, Massachusetts. His books include *The
Psychopathic God: Adolf Hitler* and *Kaiser and
Führer: A Comparative Study of Personality and Politics.* In the following essay, Waite examines the anti-
Semitic literature that flourished in Vienna during
the years Hitler lived there. According to Waite, two
writers in particular influenced the young Hitler's
opinions about race, providing him with ideas and
arguments that he would use throughout his political
career. Not only did Hitler adopt theories about race
from these authors, Waite maintains, but he also bor-
rowed from them some of the hallmarks of Nazi rule,
such as the swastika and the division of the Reich
into separate districts. Although many other factors
underlie Hitler's anti-Semitism, Waite concludes that
the intellectual concepts that Hitler discovered in
Vienna had an important and lasting impact on him.

Why did Adolf Hitler become an anti-Semite, the most vicious and historically important anti-Semite in the history of
the world? In part he became a hater of the Jews for intellectual reasons. During 1908, while he was an adolescent in
Vienna, he became impressed with the arguments of certain
anti-Semites. It was from racist pamphleteers and politicians, rather than from great figures in German intellectual
history, that Hitler drew the ideas that were so important to
his life and work. He was influenced by the mayor of Vienna,
Karl Lueger, whom he considered the greatest mayor in history, and who reached the height of his popularity as the

Excerpted from *The Psychopathic God: Adolf Hitler*, by Robert G.L. Waite. Copyright
©1977 by Robert G.L. Waite. Reprinted by permission of BasicBooks, a member of
Perseus Books, L.L.C.

young Hitler arrived from Linz. Lueger's anti-Semitism is most clearly expressed in a speech that Hitler was to echo and reecho throughout his life:

> I know only one noxious thing in this country and that is the Jewish-Liberal press. That is the dragon . . . which has put the Germans in chains and held them imprisoned. I am proud that I have already given this dragon a couple of serious wounds. I'll see to it that these wounds remain open. This dragon must be crushed so that our dear German *Volk* [folk] can be freed from its prison.

Hitler was also heavily and directly influenced by two racist pamphlet writers, Guido von List and Lanz von Liebenfels, men who reached the height of their influence during his Vienna period, 1908–1913. They are the people Hitler alluded to in his memoirs when he wrote that after having met a strange figure wearing a caftan he asked himself if this was a Jew and sought to find the answer, when, "For the first time in my life, I bought some anti-Semitic pamphlets for a few pennies."

## Hitler's Reading Material

That List and Liebenfels wrote these pamphlets seems likely for a number of reasons. First, the mystical pseudoscientific nonsense contained in their writings was exactly the type of "scientific knowledge of race" that appealed to Hitler throughout his life. Second, the pamphlets were cheap and easily obtainable in Vienna—indeed there is strong evidence that Hitler bought them and went directly to Liebenfels in 1909 to ask for and to receive, free of charge, some back copies. Third, the pamphlets were brief and dramatic and Hitler lacked the intellectual patience and discipline to read long books. . . . Finally and most importantly, both in broad outline and in details the ideas of Liebenfels and List parallel Hitler's too closely to be accidental. Liebenfels, for example, in his *Ostara* pamphlets of 1907–1910, called for a "new order" of the racially elite; he used the swastika as the symbol of racial purity; and he promised that when his new order came, stringent laws would be passed against the "mongrelization" of the Aryan race. Hitler used the same expression in promulgating his Nuremberg racial laws in 1935. Liebenfels announced that all men are divided into two groups: creative Aryans and what he called ape-men—most notably the Jews. The function of the lower race was to be slave to the Aryans. In an issue of *Ostara* of 1913 he talked about "the Holy Grail of the German blood," which must be defended by a new elite bodyguard of the racially pure. Hitler apparently liked and remembered the phrase for he told [fellow Nazi] Hermann Rauschning in the 1930's that "The problem is this: how can we arrest racial decay? . . . Shall we form . . . a select company of the really initiated? An Order, the brotherhood of Templars around *the holy grail of pure blood?*" In another pamphlet of 1908, Liebenfels an-

---

**ANTI-SEMITISM IN AUSTRIA**

*Dick Geary is a professor of modern history at the University of Nottingham in England. In the following excerpt from his book* Hitler and Nazism, *Geary explains that as an Austrian, Hitler was exposed to more prejudice against Jews than he would have been had he grown up in Germany.*

Sad as it may be, anti-semitic prejudices were far from uncommon in Austria before the First World War and certainly not the product of the deranged mind of an individual lunatic. In fact it was significant that Hitler came from Austria rather than the more western parts of Germany proper. . . . For race was an issue of much greater importance in eastern Europe, where national boundaries did not overlap with ethnic ones. The pan-German movement emerged in Austria in the late nineteenth century under the leadership of Georg von Schönerer, whose ideas had a not inconsiderable impact on the young Hitler. In part pan-Germanism, the demand for a single country for all Germans, was a response of Germans within the Austro-Hungarian Empire to the growing national awareness of other ethnic groups, among them Poles and Hungarians with a historical nationhood, and others such as Czechs and Serbs seeking at the least greater autonomy and in some cases independent nation states. The virulence of popular anti-semitism in eastern Europe was equally a response to the fact that the Jewish presence there was much more marked than in Germany, where there were no huge ghettos and where Jews constituted less than 1 per cent of the total population. Racial hatred was further fuelled in the eastern parts of Europe by the fact that many of the Jews there were unassimilated, dressed distinctly and remained loyal to their own traditions. Hitler's account of encountering a Jew on the streets of Vienna makes great play of the latter's wearing of a caftan and ring-locks.

Dick Geary, *Hitler and Nazism*, 1993.

nounced that the whole "mongrelized breed" of Jews and lesser men must be wiped off the face of the earth. In other pamphlets he urged the formation of breeding colonies and the sterilization of the weak and racially inferior. Twenty-five years later, Hitler put those ideas into practice.

## MORE ANTI-SEMITIC INFLUENCES

The Führer also took seriously the advice of Liebenfels' racist colleague and fellow anti-Semite, Guido von List. In his pamphlets of the period 1908–1914, List called for the destruction of "the hydra-headed international Jewish conspiracy"—a phrase Hitler later adopted as his own. List also argued that two things were necessary to combat the Jewish conspiracy: the establishment of a racially pure state and a global war against the international Jews who sought to destroy civilization. He devoted many pamphlets to the racially pure Reich of his dreams. The new Reich would come only when a great leader—whom List called Araharl––made his appearance. The Reich would be divided in *Gaue* [districts] and each *Gau* would have a *Gauleiter* [district leader]. Only Aryans would have citizenship rights. In a pamphlet dated 1908 List assured his readers that Aryans were superior people because the molecular structure of their blood was unique, but mainly because they had inherited certain powerful and secret Aryan symbols. These included the swastika and the runic letters, ⚡⚡. List gives a long and loving disquisition on both. The origins of the letters, S.S., are runic, he says, and stood for "*Strick Stein*" which meant—if one may condense three chapters of spurious etymology—"secret law." He urged that the guardians of the racial purity of the new Reich should wear as their insignia the racial symbol.

Clearly Hitler was influenced by other racists—no one man gave him his ideas. Dietrich Eckhart and the people of the *Thule Gesellschaft* [the Thule Society, a racist organization based in Munich], for example, were certainly important to Hitler after World War I, but they simply reinforced ideas that he got initially in Vienna during 1908–1913. Hitler must be believed when he said of his years in Vienna, "In that city I received the basis of my view of life in general and a political way of looking at things in particular which later on I had only to supplement in single instances, but which never deserted me."

## SMART POLITICS

There were other reasons why Hitler became an anti-Semite. As a consummately able political opportunist he saw, quite rightly, that it was smart politics in postwar Germany to be a Jew baiter. Indeed Hitler's establishment of the Jewish scapegoat was his greatest single political asset. He proved to those who desperately wanted to believe it that the Jews and not the Germans were responsible for all the ills that befell Germany from 1918–1933: Jews were to blame for the defeat in World War I, they were responsible for the Versailles "Treaty of Shame" and for capitalistic Western exploitation, for communism, and for the devastating inflation of 1923, and the crash of 1930, and for immorality in arts and public life. It was an effective political line.

# The First World War's Effect on Hitler

Edleff H. Schwaab

Germany's surrender in the First World War came as a shock to most Germans, and the punitive terms of the Treaty of Versailles created severe hardships for the German people in the years immediately following the war. Convinced that they could have won the war, many Germans blamed the politicians who had signed the armistice, claiming that these men had stabbed Germany in the back by surrendering at the point of victory. In the following reading, Edleff H. Schwaab writes that Adolf Hitler was among those who were deeply affected by Germany's surrender. Hitler had already formulated a vague conspiracy theory concerning a Jewish international plot to decimate Germany, Schwaab contends, and after the war he came to believe that Jewish politicians had effected Germany's surrender in order to smooth the way for a communist takeover of the nation. Schwaab concludes that Germany's loss of World War I was a primary factor in Hitler's decision to embark on a political career. Schwaab is a Boston psychologist and the author of *Hitler's Mind: A Plunge into Madness*, from which the following reading is excerpted.

When the First World War was coming to an end, Adolf Hitler was in Pasewalk Hospital near Berlin, a victim of the ever-desperate efforts of the warring nations to discover new weapons systems—in this case, poison gas. Gas warfare had become the most hideous method devised so far to kill human beings. It produced the most severe suffering of any such method, causing excruciating pains in the eyes and lungs, nausea, suffocation, and a slow choking to death.

When Hitler was temporarily blinded, the doctors who treated him were still inexperienced in the treatment of gas injuries, for there was hardly any knowledge of the effects of mustard gas behind the frontlines.

## THE MUSTARD GAS ATTACK

Hitler was in the trenches in Flanders when the British struck on the morning of October 15, 1918, at Montagne. The panicky screams of "Gas!" and the banging of big gongs sounded the alarm for a mustard gas attack. Men frantically reached for their gas masks, known to be barely effective for protection from injuries to eyes and lungs. Hitler either did not hear in time the desperate shouting of his comrades or the banging of gongs or did not succeed in fitting his gas mask in time. In any case, his eyes were injured and he was temporarily blinded. One soldier led him and other afflicted men to a field station. Within days he was on his long way back to his homeland to recuperate in a veterans' hospital at Pasewalk. Within three weeks the swelling of his eyes reduced and the irritation to his lung tissues cleared up. He regained his eyesight. On November 18, he was discharged and declared fit for service.

These three weeks at the hospital were to prove a most critical period in Hitler's life. He experienced the collapse of imperial Germany and the end of four years of a desperate war effort. Facing an uncertain future at age twenty-nine, he found himself unready for civilian life, not having acquired any skills to make a living. His intense inner drive and the increasing strength of his convictions made him decide to enter politics. In this regard, these three weeks became the beginning of a career that gradually unfolded before ending up in the excesses of another war, twenty-one years later.

## GERMANY SURRENDERS

Shortly before Hitler was wounded at Montagne, the German chiefs of staff, Generals Paul von Hindenburg and Erich Ludendorff, had reached the conclusion that the war was lost, and they advised the government to bid for an armistice. The news reached Pasewalk on November 9, 1918. The hospital chaplain addressed the wounded soldiers on November 11 to inform them with stirred emotions and tearful eyes about the end of the war and of the Reich and their Kaiser. Not only had the German High Command admitted defeat and sued for a ceasefire, but the entire structure of imperial Germany was falling apart. Navy men at the Kiel Naval Station were mutinous—a most unheard of event in the Prussian-German military tradition—and the mustachioed, saber-rattling Kaiser Wilhelm II was forced to abdicate. The symbol of Germany's nationalistic self-assertion, a man who had contributed so much to the outbreak of the Great War, he now fled into exile in Holland. He left behind a country facing the task of reorganizing itself along democratic lines by forming a republic. Seated in the small town of Weimar, the new government chose a site totally untarnished by any political or military legacy and had no more to offer than being recognized as a center of the German poetic tradition of Johann Wolfgang von Goethe.

When all this happened, Hitler was still in Pasewalk in a state of acute physical and emotional distress. After the chaplain had announced the collapse of the German war effort, Hitler broke down and cried bitterly. Until this moment he had shown a remarkable stoic quality in absorbing the turmoil of his Vienna years and the trauma of a gruesome war. The collapse of his country was more than he could take. It entailed at the same time the collapse of his own personal vision of Germany as a nation of greatness. He flung himself in tears onto his hospital cot in disbelief that all the sacrifices and sufferings of so many for so long should have been in vain. "Since the day I stood at the grave of my mother I had not cried until now," he said.

He was at the midstation of his life and, in spite of his acceptance-craving fantasies, was totally undistinguished. Had he been killed in action, he would have been but one of two million other German war dead who left no traces of their existence and simply vanished, leaving mourning mothers behind.

But he survived, and in trying to cope with the doomsday experience of a lost war, he searched for an explanation of how it was possible for such a tragedy to happen. Somebody deserved blame. Believing he had witnessed "the inhuman cruelty" of the Versailles Treaty, the floodgates of his long-suppressed, convoluted, and delusional inner world opened. In an outburst of rage over Germany's defeat, Hitler brought to the surface his latent paranoid condition. He confessed, "During those nights hatred grew in me, a hatred towards all those responsible for the deed." He labeled them "November criminals" and resolved that whoever had contributed to the collapse of Germany would have to pay a price. They were but a "gang of miserable and desperate criminals."

During the days at Pasewalk [Hitler's] conspiracy theory was reborn. All of Hitler's long-held suspicions about a Jewish international plot to destroy Germany were confirmed in his mind. A revolution had broken out, and "a couple of Jews were 'the leaders,'" whom Hitler called with derision "Orientals." He vented his fury about the very idea of a revolution, which to him was outright "madness." All his prewar images about the role Germans and Germany should play in world affairs had shattered. In his mind, only fragments of the glory of the past remained. Brooding about how to rectify this national disaster, he began to glue his thoughts together to form some kind of ideology that could serve the resurrection of his country. Slowly, he had it all worked out in his mind and eventually published his thoughts in book form in 1925, six years later.

In *Mein Kampf* Hitler recalled how he had entered the war in a state of euphoria about a unique opportunity for Germany to establish itself as a dominant power in the world. He had joyously signed up as a volunteer, thanking "Heaven with an overflowing heart for granting me the good fortunes to be permitted to live in these times." "Destiny" was taking its course, and he was convinced the war would decide "whether the German nation was to be or not to be." In his exuberance he exclaimed in a language bordering on the bizarre, "Let Heaven at last give free rein to Fate, which would be thwarted no longer. The first mighty flash of lightning struck the earth. The storm was unleashed, and the thunder of Heaven mingled with the roar of the guns of the Great War."

Such irrational enthusiasm before the shooting had started gradually yielded to frustration, rage, and anger. When it was all over, Hitler found himself in Pasewalk with his dreams of a glorious future for Germany turned into a nightmare. Chancellor Otto von Bismarck's Reich, forged with so much military cunning, had vanished. The promise of everlasting national dominance—first proclaimed in 1861 by Emanuel Geibel in the self-congratulatory arrogant message "Am deutschen Wesen soll die Welt genesen" (the spirit of Germans will help the world thrive)—had lost all sense and meaning. The epoch of imperial ambition had come to an end, inevitably and irrevocably.

To Hitler this was a catastrophic development. He was unable to accept the military defeat as a new reality facing an exhausted and war-weary nation. After all the bugles had sounded the ceasefire, he was unable to view the armistice as ushering in an era of peace; instead, he searched for support of his suspicions that the tragedy of a lost war was caused by betrayal and treachery, providing an opportunity for Jewish politicians to stoke the fires of the Bolshevik [communist] revolution in Germany. He was convinced Jews were behind the villainous plot of the Treaty of Versailles, designed as an instrument to assure permanent subjugation and dismemberment of Germany.

## GERMAN REACTIONS TO THE WAR'S END

Hitler's thoughts mirrored the sentiment of many Germans, who resented being blamed for the outbreak of the war. The war-guilt clause of the Versailles Treaty had generated an unbearable feeling of humiliation. Like the millions of other German soldiers who had trudged faithfully to the trenches feeling condemned to die for a cause only vaguely clear in their minds, Hitler believed something must have gone wrong. How else could the war have been lost? Something treacherous must have happened at the home front, way back in Germany.

These suspicions about the home front were reinforced when no welcome was extended to the returning fighting men after they had marched back from France, their heads high and feeling certain they had been undefeated on the battlefield. They had brought with them memories of terror-filled years. No one but their loved ones cared about their return, and there was nothing to prevent their alienation from civilian life. Deprived of any normal life experience for years, they did not know how to start a nonmilitary existence. For too long they had absorbed events outside the range of a peaceful human existence. Now the time for soldiering and heroism, the time of sacrifice for the Fatherland as a course of duty, suddenly held no value. All they faced were emotional scars, battle fatigue, and uncertainty about their future.

Many of these returning soldiers plunged into a continuation of violence by volunteering in the Freikorps, a kind of militia that fought intrusions of Russians and Poles into the eastern borders of Germany. The Freikorps army units had simply refused to demobilize and were led by officers who were attracted to the *völkisch* [folkish] ideas of the *völkisch* community that Germany was supposed to be.

Still others returned home fully demoralized and withdrew into a listless and shiftless pattern of life. Shell-shocked and crushed by the dramatically changed conditions of the country, they returned bewildered having fought for so long with dogged determination to wrest victory from a fatefully hopeless situation. They had been living under military discipline for years, unable to move, to eat, to sleep, or to do anything without an order. In a spirit of dejection, they became susceptible to the kind of message of hope Hitler decided to deliver by answering the questions: What next? Who would govern the country? What would the Kaiser's country become?

## HITLER'S PLANS FOR GERMANY

Hitler shared this state of desperation with his fellow Germans. He had gone to war alone and had now returned alone, having nowhere to go. The war was over, but it did not die within him. And it did not die around him either. It kept on smoldering in Russia, in Turkey, in Greece, in Syria, and in other lands. Hitler looked around and saw only ruins of the old order: failing dynasties, kings and emperors leaving empty thrones behind, and revolutions and counterrevolutions—successful in Russia but failing in Germany.

After years of hostility, the promise of peace did not meet anybody's expectations, for peace did not bring about a humane end to the deadly strain of war. Germans did not recover quickly from the feverish pitch of outright hatred, rivalry, and envy, which had reigned among the European nations for so many years before as well as during the war. During the postwar chaos it was nearly impossible to start a new era short of starting a revolution to overcome the legacy of the nineteenth century with its imperialistic expansions, colonial aggrandizements, and rabid nationalism.

Hitler meant to do exactly that, start a revolution, to topple the ruling classes with their monarchistic leaning. He also meant to start fighting the internationalism of Bolsheviks and Socialists. To him, the Weimar Republic was not an acceptable model for accomplishing such goals. The answer was a one-man rule. Disguised under the positive-sounding notion of leadership, he introduced the concept of dictatorship that Germans embraced without understanding the direction in which Hitler would lead them. In the climate of anarchy and despair, hunger and disease, inflation and unemployment, the idea of a *Führerstaat*, a law-and-order nation, did not seem to frighten them. Leadership was badly needed, and they heard Hitler declare his intention to stop the steady disintegration of German society. When Hitler set out to begin his political career in 1919, Germany was a frightfully split country, divided into the many stout, victory-minded burghers who believed in the stab-in-the-back theory to explain the causes of the national tragedy, and the war-weary hungry masses that had welcomed the end of the war with a sigh of relief. He identified with the nationalists without showing any interest in restoring the old social structure of the monarchy and was intent on continuing to fight the war against the "real enemy" who had snatched victory away from Germans at the last minute. And the real enemy was the "international Jew," whom Hitler had suspected all along of seeking fulfillment of his world-spanning ambitions by using the social and political infrastructure as a vehicle to rule.

## CHAPTER 2

# Hitler's Effect on the German People

# Hitler as a Charismatic Leader

Joseph Nyomarkay

Joseph Nyomarkay is a professor of political science at the University of Southern California in Los Angeles. He is the author of *Charisma and Factionalism in the Nazi Party*, from which the following essay is taken. According to Nyomarkay, charismatic leaders are exceptional human beings who incite such blind enthusiasm from their followers that they are able to violate laws, traditions, and even basic moral codes without repercussions. He argues that Adolf Hitler was this type of leader—a man whose unwavering belief in his own destiny impelled the German people to trust him implicitly. Both the Nazi Party members and ordinary citizens reacted to Hitler with incredibly strong emotions, and they often felt a close personal connection with their leader, Nyomarkay writes. He describes how the majority of Hitler's followers placed him on a pedestal, considering him to be almost superhuman.

A leader is charismatic if he is regarded by his followers as a person whose powers or qualities are so exceptional that they are of divine origin and inaccessible to the ordinary person. By virtue of such extraordinary, supernatural, or superhuman powers, the charismatic leader is permitted to rule. The actions of the charismatic leader can violate tradition as well as the legal framework; his legitimacy derives from his personal qualities, from his "gifts of grace," in the words of Max Weber. The significant aspect of charisma is that the extraordinary qualities of the leader are purely subjective, resting on the perception of his followers; they are not subject to any objective proof or verification. "Charisma" does not denote an objectively definable pattern of traits, nor does a

Excerpted from *Charisma and Factionalism in the Nazi Party*, by Joseph Nyomarkay. Copyright ©1967 by the University of Minnesota. Reprinted by permission of the University of Minnesota Press.

charismatic leader need to satisfy any objective, ethical, aesthetic, or other criteria. "What alone is important," writes Weber, "is how an individual is actually regarded by those subject to charismatic authority, by his followers or disciples." Charisma, as James C. Davies correctly points out, should not be considered as a "characteristic of leaders as such but [as] a relationship between leaders and followers."

## AN EXTRAORDINARY PERSON

Although charisma is subjective, resting on such qualities as the followers ascribe to the leader, it would be a mistake to assume that it could be ascribed to just anybody. There has to be a measure of extraordinariness in the person of the charismatic leader in order to evoke the enthusiasm and devotion necessary for the establishment of charismatic authority. What constitutes "extraordinariness" is of course again subjective, depending on the existing political culture, but it can hardly be doubted that a charismatic relation can be generated only by a person with some special qualities. Thus, no matter how extraordinary he may be, a person will not become a charismatic leader unless his extraordinariness is recognized by others. The transformation of extraordinariness into charisma depends on the political skills and magnetism of the potential charismatic leader and on his conviction of his historical role. A person, if he is successfully to transform extraordinariness into charisma, must take himself seriously; he must see himself as called to fulfill some historical mission. This sense of mission and its complements, the necessary political skills, are the prerequisites for the establishment of charismatic legitimacy.

Adolf Hitler took several years to transform his extraordinary personal qualities into charismatic authority in the Nazi party. According to Konrad Heiden, a contemporary German journalist, he began to take himself seriously only in the middle of the 1920's. It was in the second half of *Mein Kampf,* written after his release from prison, that he began to identify himself as the great man who "is the rarest thing to be found on this globe." He saw himself as the messiah whose mission was to realize the "absolute idea" on earth. . . .

Concomitantly with his developing sense of mission, he was employing the necessary means to generate charismatic legitimacy. The greeting "Heil Hitler" (which, significantly, was used by Hitler himself), the elaborate ceremonies of mass meetings, and the oratory, demagogy, and rituals of the party festivities were all exploited to that end.

## HITLER'S CHARISMATIC AUTHORITY

His fanatical belief in himself, his political skill in manipulating mass sentiment, and the large numbers of people who were looking for a leader and a cause enabled Hitler to become the focus of loyalty and the ultimate depository of authority in the movement by the late 1920's. He came to be obeyed by the majority of his party followers, and later by the majority of the nation, as a savior and a redeemer. Progressively, National Socialism became Hitlerism; its policies were Hitler's policies, its power was Hitler's power. By 1936 Hans Frank, Hitler's attorney, could be explicit about Hitler's charismatic authority: "There is in Germany today only one authority, and that is the authority of Führer." The charismatic nature of authority found expression in Nazi jurisprudence, which was predicated on the slogan "Führerworte haben Gesetzes Kraft" (the words of the leader have the force of law); Hitler's orders, whether oral or written, canceled all written law.

Hitler's ability to evoke strong personal attachments was important in the creation of his charismatic authority. Some revered him as a godlike man, and others followed him, according to Frank, "with a passionate enthusiasm that beclouded all reason." As G.M. Gilbert wrote, his personal influence was of such magnitude that when some old films were shown of him at Nuremberg after the war, "[Reich foreign minister Joachim von] Ribbentrop was completely overwhelmed by the voice and figure of the Führer. He wept like a baby, as if a dead father had returned to life." "The Führer had a terrifically magnetic personality," Ribbentrop told Gilbert. "You can't understand it unless you've experienced it. Do you know, even now, six months after his death, I can't completely shake off his influence?" Ernst Kaltenbrunner, head of the central office for Reich security, reacted similarly to Hitler. "Hitler's personality held an almost mesmeric fascination for him; he sincerely worshipped him and he had an unbounded faith in what he regarded as his inspired foresight and vision," William Hoettl wrote.

## EMOTIONAL REACTIONS

Hitler emerges from Joseph Goebbels's early secret diary as an extraordinary figure with whom Goebbels completely identified. His trusts and distrusts, pleasures and displeasures, presence and absence affected Goebbels deeply and intimately. He was hurt when he thought he had lost Hitler's confidence and exulted when he enjoyed his support. When in 1926 he found himself at odds with Hitler, he was crushed: "My heart aches so much . . . I have been deprived of my inner self. I am only half." When Hitler later invited him to Munich, Goebbels was as elated as a child: "I am born again . . . I am a man again . . . I am happy." And some weeks later: "I feel myself bound again at last. My last doubts are gone. *Heil Hitler.*" Goebbels loved Hitler, felt small beside him, and could not bear to be disappointed by him: "Adolf Hitler I love you, because you are great and pure at the same time."

Hitler's personality was felt not only by his immediate subordinates, but also by the mass of his followers. His capacity to make people follow him in blind fanaticism, to bring them under his spell, has been recounted by many eyewitnesses. Putzi Hanfstängl, one of Hitler's confidants, described the audience at a meeting in 1922: "I looked at the audience. Where was the nondescript crowd I had seen only an hour before? What was suddenly holding these people . . . ? The hubbub and the mugclattering had stopped and they were drinking in every word. Only a few yards away was a young woman, her eyes fastened on the speaker. Transfixed as though in some devotional ecstasy, she had ceased to be herself and was completely under the spell of Hitler's despotic faith in Germany's future greatness."

William L. Shirer, a contemporary American journalist, rendered a similar account twelve years later about the Nuremberg party rally: "About ten o'clock tonight I got caught in a mob of ten thousand hysterics who jammed the moat in front of Hitler's hotel, shouting: 'We want our Führer.' I was a little shocked at the faces, especially those of the women, when Hitler finally appeared on the balcony for a moment. They reminded me of the crazed expressions I saw once in the back country of Louisiana on the faces of some Holy Rollers who were about to hit the trail. They looked up at him as if he were a Messiah, their faces transformed into something positively inhuman."

## PEOPLE'S ATTRACTION TO HITLER

There can be little doubt that what attracted most people to National Socialism was Hitler, who could express the aspirations as well as the frustrations and the resentments of the masses. Kurt Lüdecke, a former Nazi and an acute observer of National Socialism, related his first encounter with Hitler. At that moment he knew that his long search was ended: "I had found myself, my leader and my cause . . . I had given him my soul." Goebbels reacted similarly: "From this moment I am born again, I am intoxicated." "It is impossible to describe the experience of seeing and hearing the leader for the first time," wrote one of American sociologist Theodore Abel's [German] respondents in 1934. "One thing is certain: from that day on I had no other purpose than to fight for him until victory was won." "In July the leader came to Tilsit," wrote another. "I saw him for the first time. . . . Those hours are never to be forgotten. The leader spoke. For the first time I heard his voice. His words went straight to the heart. From now on my life and efforts were dedicated to the leader. I wanted to be a true follower."

Further examples would only belabor the point that Hitler's followers regarded him as more than an ordinary leader. Even such a cynical member of his inner circle as Hermann Göring admitted as much after the war. It is not an exaggeration to conclude from the depositions and memoirs of Nazi followers that for them Hitler was a person of extraordinary gifts beyond ordinary men. He possessed the confidence of the masses who "surrendered to him with hysterical enthusiasm . . . and followed him with a mad jubilation" (as Hans Frank told Gilbert). He was the tribune of the people, possessing their souls and giving their life a new meaning. There is little doubt that for the majority of his followers he was the movement and the idea—in short, he was the source of legitimacy.

# Hitler's Oratorical Skills

William Carr

Most people believe that Adolf Hitler became a ranting, hysterical madman during his impassioned speeches, a popular assumption that has been bolstered by specific film clips of Hitler's wild gestures. However, William Carr argues that these brief images only capture a small part of Hitler's oratorical style. In actuality, he contends, Hitler was a masterful public speaker who employed a variety of oratorical techniques and was particularly expert at gauging and responding to the mood of the audience. As Hitler rose in power and prestige, Carr explains, he introduced grand and emotionally stirring pageantry to his public speeches. Hitler's finely crafted oratorical skills, combined with his knowledge of mass psychology, allowed him to effectively manipulate his listeners, the author concludes. Carr taught for many years at the University of Sheffield in England and wrote *Hitler: A Study in Personality and Politics*, from which the following reading is excerpted.

Historians still find difficulty in writing dispassionately about a man whose deeds were written in blood across the face of wartime Europe from the Atlantic coastline to the Russian steppes. The crimes for which Adolf Hitler and his associates were rightly held responsible still deserve dishonourable mention today in a world grown daily more accustomed to violence and untimely death. All the same, while no one would seek to minimize the enormity of these crimes against humanity, many of those who lived through this tumultuous period will continue to remember Hitler not primarily as the main instigator of the mass murders at the death camps of Maidenek, Sobidor and Treblinka . . . but first and foremost as the popularist orator and firebrand who cast a spell over millions of Germans desperately seeking reassurance at a time of unprecedented crisis, a spell which for many of them was not broken until enemy armies swept into the Third Reich in 1945.

## A GREAT ORATOR

By any objective standard Hitler must rank as one of the great orators of history, perhaps the greatest in the twentieth century. Others have surpassed him by the brilliance of their verbal dialectics, many by the originality of their arguments, and nearly all by the broad humanity of their message. Yet surely no one ever mastered the art of public speaking so thoroughly or exploited the shifting moods of audiences with greater skill than Hitler. As this was, perhaps, the most obvious expression of the man, it would seem an appropriate point at which to commence an examination of Hitler's personality.

At the very outset we are confronted by a dense thicket of mythology which has grown up around the person of Adolf Hitler. The popular image familiar to millions through the media of the cinema and television is of a ranting mob orator, a demoniacal figure carried away by the elemental power of his own oratory and utterly incapable of controlling his own emotions. Film extracts from the 1930s have contributed to this false picture by showing Hitler—invariably for a few seconds only—shouting at the top of his voice, gesticulating, head thrown back, eyes raised to heaven, features distorted, sweat pouring down his face and back, his raucous tones reverberating round the hall while a brown-shirted rally responds ecstatically to his unrestrained outpourings. From this picture one is left to infer either that Germans are peculiarly vulnerable to hysterical oratory, or else that Hitler was an unsophisticated rabble-rouser who relied on unusually strong lungs to captivate an audience—or possibly a combination of both.

Almost exactly the reverse is the truth. Sophistication in the use of the techniques of public speaking and care in the preparation of speeches were the hallmarks of his oratory. No one worked harder or in a more calculating manner to win the hearts of an audience. In public he spoke always by design and rarely by accident. His speeches, like those of his great antagonist, Winston Churchill, were always well-structured and thought out in considerable detail. But unlike the generality of German politicians before and after the Third Reich, Hitler did not read out his speeches word for word, or at any rate not in the early years. He was far too astute a psychologist not to appreciate the debilitating effect written perorations have on the rapport between speaker and audience. Having an exceptionally retentive memory, he could convey an impression of spontaneity and freshness however long he spoke, and with no more than a few notes on the rostrum containing key phrases to remind him of the sequence of his argument.

## HITLER'S STYLE AS A PUBLIC SPEAKER

One should remember, too, that Hitler's earliest oratorical triumphs were achieved with a minimum of pageantry. In the early days when he was struggling for recognition, a table top in a beer hall was his only platform, his dress not the ill-fitting brown uniform, ungainly jack boots and unflattering peak cap of later years but the modest nondescript garb of the man in the street—dark suit, white shirt and black tie. In the rough-and-tumble atmosphere of the rowdy Munich beer kellers he proved his mettle as an orator without the pomp and circumstance of later years. He did not rant and rave all the time—a physical impossibility for a man who spoke normally two hours and more—but addressed his audiences in quiet tones at first, even hesitantly, developing his chosen theme with occasional shafts of humour and invariably with lucidity and skill. Unlike many public speakers of those days he could deal expertly with hecklers. During the discussion periods—which in the early days invariably followed his speech—he stood with folded arms listening to opponents before dispatching them with a few well-chosen and sometimes humorous words. Only later did the Brown shirts save him the trouble, though from the start Hitler's audiences were never particularly tolerant and often shouted opponents down.

Hitler took immense pains over the minutiae of his oratory. Take, for example, the extravagant and theatrical gestures at which he excelled—the clenched fists, the admonitory forefinger pointing now at the audience, now heavenwards, and the outstretched arms. Histrionic gestures of this kind were something of a novelty for German audiences; political speakers either did not gesticulate or, if they did, gave little or no thought to the effect of awkward gestures on their audiences. Hitler went to endless trouble over such details. He is said to have studied the technique of Ferdl Weiss, a popular Munich comedian, for capturing the attention of noisy beer-hall crowds before commencing his act. According to Konrad Heiden, an early biographer of Hitler, he practised his gestures diligently in front of a mirror in his shabby room in Munich's Thierschstrasse. He also had the party photographer, Heinrich Hoffmann, snap him in action so that he could study each gesture minutely. Only those passing the most severe scrutiny were employed on public platforms. It was equally characteristic that he studied in great detail the acoustics of the major beer halls in Munich and adjusted the pitch of his voice to suit each one. Once the party grew in size and Hitler was firmly established as leader, he paid much attention to the external trappings of meetings as part of a calculated attempt to heighten the emotional experience and to lower the mental resistance of the audience.

### The Use of Pageantry

A typical example of the changing style of Hitler's oratory was the Zirkus Krone meeting in March 1927, where he addressed his first public gathering since the removal of the ban on public speaking imposed on him in 1923. As usual he was billed to speak at 8 o'clock in the evening. It was never his practice to appear punctually. Instead he remained in his room pacing up and down going over his speech (usually composed a few hours before). By telephone he kept in touch with the meeting, ringing at frequent intervals to ascertain the size and political complexion of the crowd. By 8.00 the Zirkus Krone was half-full. On the swastika-draped platform a military band was playing the old familiar tunes setting the feet tapping while a sprinkling of uniformed Brown shirts chatted to friends in the audience. At 8.30 Hitler strode in, having delayed long enough to arouse expectancy but not long enough to arouse hostility towards the unpunctual speaker. Greeted with rapturous applause by a crowd of some 8,000, he walked briskly to the platform surrounded by his henchmen. A trumpet sounded and a hush fell on the crowd. Through the hall marched the Brown shirts, preceded by two rows of drummers and by the 'blood flag'—the banner carried in the march to Munich's Feldherrnhalle during the abortive putsch of 1923 and stained with the blood of fallen comrades. The audience greeted the flag with shouts of *Heil* while Hitler stood arm outstretched (a salute he picked up from the Italian fascists) at the rostrum until all were seated. The stage was set; the audience, reassured by the parade of party strength, their emotions aroused by the banners and uniforms, listened to the Führer full of expectancy. With the party firmly established, if only on a local base, Hitler avoided anything likely to fracture the rapport between perspiring orator and ecstatic audience. Discussion time had gone for good, partly because of the intrinsic difficulty of organizing discussion at a mass meeting, but primarily because the Hitler of the late 1920s was consciously cultivating a different public image—that of the Führer rallying the faithful for the long haul ahead, not the agitator goading the masses into rebellion. At the end of the speech, which usually ended in a great emotional crescendo, Hitler strode out theatrically into the night to the thunderous applause of the audience brought to its feet as the band struck up the *Deutschlandlied.*

Once the Nazis were in power the pageantry grew more impressive and ostentatious, culminating in the great party rallies at Nuremberg, the old imperial city. For eight days each year the high drama of the party rally was enacted against the magnificent setting of a medieval town with all the sophisticated paraphernalia of mass propaganda at the organizers' disposal. The meeting of the *Gauleiter* or regional party leaders in the middle of rally week was an excellent example of brilliant staging. Tens of thousands of party members gathered in the evening in the Zeppelinwiese to await the Führer. To the roar of applause and illuminated by a circle of one hundred hidden searchlights, the Führer entered the vast arena. At the head of a procession of high party officials he walked slowly down the steps and up to the tribune to the accompaniment of thunderous applause. When silence fell at last on the arena, thousands of Nazi banners moved forward through the serried ranks while searchlights picked out the golden eagles on the red standards, a superbly impressive setting for the speech that followed.

## PERSONAL MAGNETISM

Yet, when all is said and done, oratory has a gossamer-like magic about it that defies precise analysis. Skilful techniques and a receptive audience are essential ingredients of success but the indispensable element is the personal magnetism of the speaker. Though Hitler clearly experienced great difficulty with ordinary human relationships, was rarely completely at ease outside the immediate circle of party cronies and established few if any intimate relationships, on public occasions and in front of an audience private inhibitions rolled away and he became literally a man transformed. A Hitler speech was superb theatre—at any rate for those who liked old-fashioned melodrama. Hitler was his own script writer, choreographer and actor-manager rolled into one. With uncanny skill he exploited the whole register of human emotions. Contrary to popular belief he did not lack a certain sense of humour either in public or in private; some of the speeches in the late 1920s and early 1930s attacking republican politicians still make entertaining reading provided that one does not lose patience with a speaker whose mordant wit was always at the expense of opponents and never at his own. And however preposterous his premises seem to rational men, it has to be admitted that he could argue a case cleverly and on occasions persuasively.

It would, however, be grossly misleading to suppose that Hitler's speeches were designed primarily to appeal to the intelligence or good humour of his audiences. Nothing could be further from the truth. Hitler's aim in the early years was quite simply to arouse and mobilize the emotions of his audience—the noble and the ignoble alike—as a means of bringing the Nazi Party to power. There is no doubt that he had a firm grasp of the principles of mass psychology. More than most politicians he was acutely aware that civilization is only skin deep, that primitive emotions lie very close to the surface of ordinary people, and that these instincts can be most effectively manipulated at mass meetings held in the evening when mental resistance is low. As he remarked with revealing candour in a well-known passage in *Mein Kampf:*

> When from his little workshop or big factory in which he [the individual] feels very small, he steps for the first time into a mass meeting and has thousands and thousands of people of the same opinion around him . . . he is swept away by three or four thousand others into the mighty effect of suggestive intoxication and enthusiasm, when the visible success and agreement of thousands confirm to him the rightness of the new doctrine and for the first time arouse doubt in the truth of his previous conviction—then he himself has succumbed to the magic influence of mass . . . suggestion. The will, the longing, and also the power of thousands are accumulated in

every individual. The man who enters such a meeting doubting and wavering leaves it inwardly reinforced: he has become a link in the community.

Hitler's blend of dogmatic assertion, repetition, biting sarcasm and emotional appeal usually did the trick. By the time he reached the end of the two hours' speech, the audience was applauding frequently. Applause, as a contemporary recalled, seemed to inspire a veritable torrent of words in him and his voice rose to a crescendo. Yet always he remained 'ice cold', never carried away by the enthusiasm he engendered. He waved applause down and continued quietly never losing his place, continuing to build up his arguments pyramid-like before the eyes of his audience as his voice moved from *pianissimo* through *fortissimo* to *furioso*. To that extent his speeches were always contrived and never spontaneous. But what really counted was his remarkable ability to persuade an audience that he was in deadly earnest. So when the spellbinder released them, the people streamed homewards—or occasionally marched shoulder to shoulder into the centre of Munich singing patriotic songs and shouting anti-semitic slogans—their prejudices confirmed, their hopes rekindled by a man who identified himself with their fears and aspirations and in masterful fashion promised to realize their deepest desires.

# Hitler Exploited Economic and Political Conditions to Increase His Popularity

Horst von Maltitz

In the following article, taken from his book *The Evolution of Hitler's Germany: The Ideology, the Personality, the Moment,* Horst von Maltitz asserts that Hitler might never have gained political power in Germany had it not been for certain economic and political conditions that occurred after the First World War. He explains that during the period when Hitler was first becoming politically active, German society was under intense stress. The punitive Treaty of Versailles—which required Germany to make exorbitant reparation payments to the victors of the war—and the financial devastation of the Great Depression created an economic crisis that severely affected most Germans. Von Maltitz also examines the political situation, writing that the Weimar Republic (Germany's first democratic government) bore the brunt of the blame for the nation's economic woes and shattered pride. Germans longed for a strong, decisive leader to guide them through their rough times, the author maintains, and this climate eventually allowed Hitler to establish himself as a dictator.

Even a man of Adolf Hitler's ability, determination, and ideological convictions would not have been able to establish himself in Germany as a dictator of unprecedented power, had he not encountered a constellation of political, economic, and sociopsychological conditions and developments during the period from 1919 to 1933, which were singularly favorable to the impact of his personality and to the assertion of the ideology which he could present. What he found when the army discharged him in 1919 was a historical catastrophe: a defeated nation being deeply humiliated by the victors; domestic political turbulence, if not chaos; disunity; economic disorder or disaster; and a people in despair. It was precisely the soil in which demagoguery, lust for power, and a sadistic destructive personality could prosper. It was also the condition in which the defeated but still proud nation was apt eagerly to respond to an ideology that told it of its fundamental greatness, its superiority over all others; explained away the causes of the defeat or the defeat itself; and described with apparent certainty a program by which the nation could emerge from disaster into health and into a glory greater, in fact, than anything the country had known before in history. It is reasonably certain that Hitler would never have accomplished his breakthrough without at least two external factors (if not more): the desperate economic conditions and the continuing humiliations of Germany by the Allied Powers even after the conclusion of the Peace of Versailles. In fact, the very terms of the peace treaty furnished Hitler with some of his most effective ammunition. Abnormal times seemed to call for an abnormal man and his abnormal solutions. This was the moment in history for him and for the ideology of National Socialism.

## THE ECONOMIC SITUATION

The date of birth of the Weimar Republic might be said to be February 6, 1919, when its National Assembly opened in that city. This coincided roughly with what Hitler called "my first more or less purely political activity." The five or six years which followed were probably the most turbulent period in modern German history—politically as well as economically. Hitler himself contributed relatively little to that turbulence. He was still a comparatively unknown agitator who received more attention from the Munich police and the courts than from the general public. Most people still did not take him seriously.

Politically the first few years of the Weimar Republic were characterized by violent domestic struggles, bloodshed in many cities, a succession of weak central and local governments, widespread refusal to accept their authority, crime, and general disorder. Economically the blockade of Germany by the Allied Powers was continuing, and with it the general starvation or undernourishment which had begun during the war. Business stagnated and unemployment was severe. The discharged soldiers, some still armed, were roaming the streets in tattered uniforms, unable to find anything to do and to fit themselves into an orderly civilian society. But it was also a time when a small number of clever business operators succeeded in making large profits out of the general chaos.

The economy of this early period after World War I was dominated by the problem of the so-called reparation payments which the Treaty of Versailles required Germany to make to the victorious powers. The impoverished economy of the country found it difficult or impossible to meet these very large payments, for the transfer of which, at any rate, it was unable to earn enough foreign currency by exports. Government after government fell over the issue of these payments. The crisis deepened when, in January 1923, the French and Belgian governments decided to have their troops occupy the German Ruhr district to obtain payment by force from the profitable heavy industry of that area, and from German customs duties. But the population of the district adopted an attitude of passive resistance and became a financial charge on the already overburdened central government, which, incompetent as it seemed to be, saw no remedy other than to print new money. The result was the wildest, most uncontrolled inflation in the history of any country. By June, 1923, the mark was quoted at 150,000 to the dollar; on July 30, at 1 million; on November 20, at 4.2 *billion.* In other words, the mark was really no longer worth anything, and there was monetary chaos. In the wild days of November, 1923, a worker's pay check which, at the beginning of the week, might still have paid for rent and food, would, at the end of the week, do no more than buy a postage stamp. Manufacturing was near a standstill, and farmers failed to ship their products to the cities.

At long range, the situation was severely aggravated by an unfortunate decision of the German Supreme Court which held that "a mark equals a mark," in other words, that, for example, 100,000 of the completely devalued mark of 1923 was good tender in payment of a debt in that amount which dated back to the days of the gold mark before 1918. Thus a mortgage of 100,000 or 1,000,000 marks could be paid off with a postage stamp. Savings accounts were wiped out.

Later a revaluation law restored a small percentage of the losses in some situations, but the financial damage that had been done to large population groups, especially the middle classes, remained severe and frequently irreparable.

There followed a difficult period of deflation. The currency was finally stabilized, but business conditions remained uncertain with much unemployment and general poverty. Moreover, the extensive political unrest, which bordered on civil war, was not conducive to an improvement in the economy. Slowly, however, the situation eased. The reparation terms were lightened, the Ruhr mines and the customs duty collections were returned to German hands, and in January, 1926, the last French troops were withdrawn. The economy was far from prospering, but it was at least functioning; and by 1928 unemployment amounted to no more than 1,624,000.

## THE GREAT DEPRESSION

Not long thereafter, however, the worldwide Great Depression struck; and it came as a particularly heavy blow to a country which had hardly recovered from inflation and deflation and was still convalescing. It had few, if any, reserves. Unemployment climbed to 3,217,608 in January, 1930; to 4,886,925 in January, 1931; to 6,041,010 in January, 1932; and it stood at 6,013,612 in January, 1933, two months before Hitler came to power. This was a very considerable number of unemployed in a country whose total population was only about 60 million with an estimated total labor force of about 20 million. In an industrial city like Berlin, only about 40 percent of the possible jobs were available, but unemployment insurance for a worker with a wife and two children amounted to about $4.25 per week.

Hitler took full political advantage of the general misery. Beginning in the early days of his political career to the day of his seizure of power (and even thereafter) he never ceased hammering away at the theme that "the system"—meaning democracy and the Jews—was responsible for all the economic disasters, and that determined leadership, such as he was able to give, would quickly guide the country into stability and prosperity. And in this respect, he did not really have to do much persuading. If there was any tipping of a scale, it was the Great Depression that tipped it in Hitler's favor. By and large, the people and even many politicians, party leaders, writers, and others were quite ready to identify the economic disasters with their new democratic form of government. The two, after all, had coincided in point of time, and no one had had previous experience with democracy. At any rate, in times of desperate economic crises, unemployment, and even starvation, a great many affected people cannot be reached by rational argument; and in a state of exhaustion or helplessness, they will not be very particular in their choice of means of relief. It was a fertile field for Hitler.

## Downward Mobility

The groups which had been most severely affected by the inflation and the subsequent economic crises were the lower middle class and the middle class. They had lost most or all of their savings and much of their social prestige. Many small businesses had gone bankrupt. Some members of these groups had been forced to move down into the proletariat, and others were in imminent danger of having to do so. To all, their new poverty looked like a profound disgrace. There was, in fact, an atmosphere of social panic in these groups. It was not surprising, then, that these were the groups which were to become the backbone of the National Socialist Movement. . . .

When Hitler came to power in March 1933, more than 6 million were unemployed. By October of that year, the number was reduced to 3,744,860. By 1936, unemployment had been eliminated. The small businesses of the lower middle class, moreover, had been rehabilitated. In part, this highly significant success was due to the rearmament policy and other measures of the regime; in part, it was due to the worldwide lifting of the Great Depression. But no matter what the causes were, those millions of Germans who had finally been rescued from misery and had been given security were inclined to see Hitler as their savior; and from then on, not surprisingly, they were willing to put their trust in him.

## The Political Situation

Culturally, the Weimar Republic was magnificent while it lasted. It represented a splendid late flowering of a true civilization, as Germany may never see again. The "Golden Twenties" were perhaps more golden in the Weimar Republic than anywhere else. There were architect Walter Gropius and the Bauhaus [school of design], which changed the face of the world; there was *The Magic Mountain* of Thomas Mann and much other outstanding literature; there were painters like Paul Klee, Wassily Kandinsky, George Grosz, and the whole expressionist school; there were the theater of Max Reinhardt and the plays of Bertold Brecht; German films were opening up a new world of art; Albert Einstein changed the world of physics. But it was a kind of feverish life of the mind. Peter Gay calls it "a dance on the edge of a volcano." It coexisted closely with extreme turbulence in politics and economics, with misery, deprivation, injustice,

### HITLER'S PROMISE OF ORDER

*D. Jablow Hershman and Julian Lieb are the authors of* A Brotherhood of Tyrants: Manic Depression and Absolute Power. *In the following excerpt, they describe some of the reasons Hitler gained popularity during the troubled times Germany experienced after World War I.*

Part of the explanation of Hitler's popularity lies in Germany's historical situation—the agonizing humiliation of defeat in World War I, a subsequent siege of economic chaos that pauperized the middle class, and a faction-rent government that inspired no confidence. The Germans were accustomed to autocracy and many felt that democracy had delivered the nation to disaster. Hitler's promise of order—and his strong opposition to communism—had enormous appeal to conservative groups, including many clergymen, educators, civil servants, military officers, and industrialists.

He also appeared to the lower classes who sensed that Hitler, a failure during the formative years of his life, was the Teutonic little man, troubled by the same fears and yearnings as his fellow citizens. To the young, Hitler was a hero offering them a purpose in life—the greatness of Germany. To others he appeared as a father offering what Germans had learned to value most in life: security. A follower of Hitler said: "Why do the Germans love Hitler? Because with Adolf Hitler they feel safe!" Moreover, many Germans who voted Hitler into power expected him to be sobered by the responsibilities of government, to forget his wilder promises, and to mature into the traditional leader they desired.

D. Jablow Hershman and Julian Lieb, *A Brotherhood of Tyrants: Manic Depression and Absolute Power*, 1994.

and many political murders. It almost seemed that the creative restless culture of Weimar, while self-absorbed and introspective, fed in some mysterious way on the decay of its surroundings. And when it all ended with Hitler's seizure of power, "the exiles [Gay says] were the greatest collection of transplanted intellect, talent and scholarship the world has ever seen."

Politically, the life and death of the Weimar Republic was deeply affected by two untruths or lies. One was the dogma of the *Kriegsschuldlüge*, that is, the doctrine that Germany carried no guilt at all for the outbreak of World War I, but that the war was forced upon the Germans by their enemies. The other lie was the legend of the traitorous "stab in the back" by which the unbeaten German army was deprived of victory in 1918.

## A WIDELY HELD BELIEF

It was surprising to what extent the war-guilt-lie became unshakable dogma. The dogma was official policy of all successive Weimar governments, just as it represented the privately held opinion of 99 percent of the people. Dinning it into the head of every school child was an important function of the teaching profession, and the whole effort was thoroughly successful. Virtually no one questioned the dogma. Hitler's tirades merely repeated what everyone was convinced was the truth.

Had this not been German dogma, which for about forty years was not even subject to examination, the political views and emotions of a good many Germans would have been very different. If the German cause in World War I was not just but unjust, then the defeat in the war would not have seemed to be an undeserved blow of fate; and even the alleged traitors—Hitler's "November criminals"—who executed the legendary stab in the back might not have seemed quite so wicked. The loss of the war might not have been felt as quite so monstrous an injustice of fate, so that less resentment and hatred would have resulted. Above all, the very harsh terms of the Treaty of Versailles (while still far too harsh to be compatible with the generosity of a truly wise victor) might not seem wholly unjustified. And if there had been any kind of moral justification for the Versailles terms in German eyes, then much of the ideological underpinnings of aggressive German nationalism and later of National Socialism would have been knocked away. Strange to say, in retrospect it looks as if the dogma of the war-guilt-lie, which the Weimar Republic itself so ardently propagated, carried in it some of the seeds of Weimar's destruction. In thousands of speeches and proclamations, and in his writings, Hitler never ceased to hammer away at the infamy, disgrace, dishonor, and shame of Versailles. With him this was an entirely basic tenet and a most useful propaganda tool. At any rate, to millions of Germans the Treaty of Versailles looked like ample, new justification for all the traditional deep-seated aversion against the West.

## THE FALSE LEGEND

Even more important was the second lie with which the Weimar Republic had to live: the legend that Germany was never militarily defeated in World War I and that the war was lost merely because of a stab in the back by traitors. . . . The legend was, however, never as widely believed as the dogma of the war-guilt-lie. The Left denied it; in the Center, some did and some did not believe it; and the Right took it for its gospel. But, at any rate, none of the various Weimar governments ever made a determined effort to disprove it. The legend thus created a serious permanent split down the middle of the nation. Large parts of the population were unwilling to acquiesce in the defeat and regarded it as the fruit of national disloyalty. To them, acquiescence, like the stab in the back itself, remained un-German, and the legend did not let them rest. All kinds of groups, large and small, crackpots and respectable, continued to agitate for action to undo the defeat. Hitler's Movement was one of them, and ultimately all others merged or were forced to merge into it.

One of the worst results of the legend was that somehow the Weimar Republic and with it democracy in general were identified with the loss of the war and thus became objects of hatred and contempt. Large parts of the nation were never willing to recognize Weimar as a legitimate political entity, any more than they were willing to acknowledge the military defeat. Hitler and National Socialism grew out of this hatred, out of this emotionally conceived lack of a legitimate government, and in a sense they were thus a product of World War I.

The two lies poisoned the body of the nation; no nation

could have been healthy with them long. It was not until long after the end of the Second World War, if then, that the Germans learned to face the true facts of World War I or lost interest in them. Had they faced them in 1918, the Weimar Republic might have been saved; there might have been no Hitler.

# Hitler's Appeal to Young Germans

Robert G.L. Waite

In the following selection, Robert G.L. Waite examines the overwhelming support that the youth of Germany gave to Adolf Hitler. In particular, Waite looks
at the common experiences shared by this generation, who were small children during World War I
and the Great Depression. He points out that during
their childhood, this generation suffered greatly from
malnutrition, starvation, fear, and anxiety. In addition, he writes, most of these children felt abandoned
by fathers who were away fighting in the war—or
who never returned from the front. The economic
distress and national humiliation that followed the
war further traumatized this generation, Waite states.
As they grew older, these young people were en-
tranced by Hitler's promise of a revitalized Germany
and even saw Hitler as the father figure so longed for
during the war years, according to the author. Waite
is a professor emeritus of history from Williams College in Williamstown, Massachusetts, and the author
of *The Psychopathic God: Adolf Hitler*, from which
the following selection is excerpted.

Members of Adolf Hitler's own generation, born in the
1890s, gave him broad support whether they were shop-
keepers or journalists, soldiers or peasants, priests or professors. But those who turned to him with particular fervor
were the sons and daughters of this generation—those, born
during and shortly after the Great War, who would become
the radical youth of 1930–1933. These young people were of
the utmost importance to Hitler, and he responded to their
needs so effectively that one historian of the Weimar youth
movement concluded, "National Socialism came to power as

the party of youth." Statistics bear him out: of all Germans in the 18–30 age group who were members of political parties, over 42 percent had joined the Nazis by 1932, compared with less than 20 percent in the Social Democratic Party. In Hamburg, 66 percent of the Party members were younger than 30; in Halle the percentage was 86 percent. In the Reichstag, 60 percent of the National Socialists were under 40; among the Social Democrats only 10 percent were of that age group.

## HITLER'S DRAWING POWER

It was symptomatic of a rising trend that even before Hitler achieved sweeping success at the polls, the official German Students' Association in 1931 elected a fanatic Nazi as its president. Hitler's drawing power for youth was remarkable. One Sunday in 1932 more than 100,000 young people came to hear him speak in Berlin and marched past him for seven-and-a-half hours.

The sheer numbers of youth were impressive. So was their aggressiveness. As one writer [Peter Merkl] concluded, "It was evidently the good luck of the Nazi movement to become the chief beneficiary of an *enormous, destructive tidal wave* in the ebb and flow of the generations." Why were these young people so peculiarly attracted to Hitler and his primitive program of calculated hatred and aggression? What forces made this the most violent generation in German history? Why precisely in the years 1930–1933 did so many students turn to Hitler? Peter Loewenberg, trained in both history and psychoanalysis, has suggested that answers may be found by combining our knowledge of the two disciplines: psychoanalysis, which supplies an understanding of personality function, and the "cohort theory" of generational change, developed by cultural anthropologists and social historians.

## CHILDHOOD TRAUMAS

Surely *external* historical forces—an authoritarian tradition, an ethos that denigrated democracy, and the economic and social consequences of inflation and depression—are important to an understanding of the rise of Hitler. But so too is an understanding of individual personal experience and psychological development. In studying these young people who proclaimed Hitler their Führer and savior, Loewenberg has found a direct and important connection between anxieties and hatreds experienced during the Great Depression and infantile experiences associated with the Great War and its aftermath. The Great Depression served, in psychoanalyst Sigmund Freud's term, as an "external disturbance" which triggered reversion to a childhood trauma. In this instance, the trauma was World War I, a time when this generation, as infants, experienced fear, hunger, feelings of abandonment, and longing for the return of an idealized soldier-father. The renewed trauma of 1930–1933 evoked in this "Nazi Youth Cohort" the political response of welcoming Hitler because he fulfilled the psychological needs both of early childhood experience and the renewed crisis of adolescence.

The term "cohort" is used rather than "generation" because a group attains identity and psychological cohesion not as a result of the date of their birth but because it has shared a significant psychological experience. As Robert Jay Lifton has shown in his studies of the survivors of Hiroshima, the entire group—regardless of age—suffered similar psychological reactions. Similarly, the concentration camp experience marked for life all those who survived. Although a major catastrophe has an effect on all ages, it will have the greatest influence on the very young because their personalities are the most malleable. World War I was such an event for those who later turned to Hitler. Broadly speaking, the war affected most deeply two age groups: the generation born in the period of 1890–1900, which participated in the prewar youth movement, the *Fronterlebnisse* [frontline soldiers] of the war, and the Free Corps movement; and their children of the Nazi Youth Cohort. Much too young to have fought in the war, they were not too young to have been scarred by it. Most notably they remembered hunger. Dozens of memoirs of this generation recall prolonged and gnawing hunger as the first terrible memory of childhood. To take only one illustration, a German friend told American novelist Pearl Buck how vividly she remembered as a little girl that during 1916–1917 her family collected nettles to boil as a vegetable, and that once, when she was sick, she had the glorious—but guilty—experience of drinking, ever so slowly, a whole glass of milk all by herself.

## HUNGER AND VIOLENCE

Hunger increased after the armistice, as the Allies continued the blockade until Germany accepted the Versailles Treaty.

The birth-weights of babies went down alarmingly. Mothers were unable to nurse, and cow's milk—when available— was lacking in fats and vitamins. Schoolchildren of those years showed a marked increase in bed-wetting and "nervous disorders." A hardened British war correspondent reported from Cologne in 1919: "Although I have seen many horrible things in the world, I have seen nothing so pitiful as these rows of babies feverish from want of food, exhausted by privation to the point that their little limbs are like slender wands, their expression hopeless and their faces full of pain." An American historian [William L. Langer] who was a student in Germany in 1921 recalls being asked over and over, "How could you, a civilized human being, withhold food from us after the fighting had stopped?" Hunger, coupled with anxiety and fear, produced in these children feelings of hostility, hatred, and aggression. Normally, society requires that children repress such feelings, but the war atmosphere actually encouraged destructive impulses.

Children tend to reflect the attitudes of the society in which they live. The sales of toy bombing planes and machine guns, for example, declined in America each Christmas between 1971 and 1973 while the United States was committing what parents increasingly came to believe were outrages against the people of Vietnam and Cambodia. On the other hand, in Northern Ireland sales of war games and guns increased during the same years. In Germany during World War I, children learned a kind of "primitive idealization": the world was either all good (German) or all bad (the Enemy). The Enemy was to be hated, feared, and killed. Thus, instead of repressing destructive impulses and turning away from horror and hatred, children turned "toward them with primitive excitement," as Loewenberg writes.

### FEELINGS OF ABANDONMENT

The Nazi Youth Cohort, during their wartime infancy, must have felt abandoned when their mothers, by the thousands, left their traditional roles in nursery, kitchen, and church to work in armament factories. One of the most remarkable social facts in German history is the statistic that in Prussia by 1917 there were 500 percent more women working in industry than in 1913, and 1,000 percent more serving as railway workers.

As children, members of the Cohort tended to have an

ambivalent attitude toward their absent fathers. They were idolized as heroes who would certainly save the Fatherland and return in glory. But there must also have been resentment and hostility toward a father who had left his children alone for so long with their mother. Child psychologists have demonstrated that when fathers are absent for protracted periods, Oedipal desires increase, along with guilt feelings and hostility toward the absent father. Such feelings of guilt, mixed with separation anxiety, often result in rage and aggression, which may break out in later periods of life: witness the excesses of the Free Corps, which thousands of the older Cohort joined, and the violent aggressive tendencies many contemporaries observed among the young adults of the Great Depression.

It is true, of course, that in other belligerent countries mothers and fathers left home and children felt neglected. But two facts made a critical difference in the German experience and had a significant effect on the Nazi Youth Cohort in the days of their early childhood: first, they suffered persistent hunger not experienced in the countries of the Entente; second, the German father, if he returned home at all, came back in defeat and not as a hero. Further, in Germany the traditional authoritarian father-figure of the emperor had fled and abandoned his people. The Revolution provided no one to take his place.

The children of the Cohort had other experiences that seared their memories: defeat was followed by near starvation and revolution. The Versailles Treaty added to the syndrome, for it made all Germans—including the young—formally responsible for all the disasters of the war. The inflation of 1923 reinforced the conviction that fathers had failed to provide order and security. The frustrations and fears and hunger of the Great Depression reawakened infant memories of hunger in 1919 and 1916–1917—hunger that evoked aggressive and destructive impulses.

## HITLER AS A FATHER FIGURE

It is not nearly enough to make the general comment that German youth were attracted to Hitler because he was "an authoritarian figure who offered a radical program." Young Germans were drawn to Hitler for *very specific reasons.* He alone, among all the political leaders of the postwar world, responded to their particular, deeply felt psychological needs. He was the incarnation of the idealized father-Führer they had imagined during the disturbing years of their infancy; he was what they had always hoped their own fathers would be—"the unknown hero of the trenches" who returned in glory wearing the Iron Cross First Class. He was a soldier-leader who promised to establish a military state where children and adults would wear uniforms and march in purposeful, disciplined ranks. They could swear an oath of total fidelity to this deified and distant Führer and help him build a resurgent and powerful German nation. The very fact that Hitler looked so average and nondescript and that so little was known about his personal life helped to strengthen the image of the father substitute. For their own fathers were average Germans who had been absent so long as to become strangers to their children.

It is difficult to convey the depths of desire young Germans felt in the postwar years for a father-Führer they could believe in and follow. A lead article in a national student magazine for January 1924 sent forth "a call for the Führer" who would have "faith in himself, in us, and in his mission." Students at Göttingen University as early as July 1920 proclaimed, "We are *consumed* with *longing* for a great Führer. . . ." The Protestant Association of University Students expressed the same hope: "*A cry from the heart* responds to an *urgent, pent-up demand* that lives within all of us . . . for the coming of the Führer of our people."

Young women of the Cohort also found Adolf Hitler to be the father-image of their dreams. Two sisters born in 1913 and 1915 recalled that their earliest memory was of their mother wearing black and weeping over their missing father. They found it impossible to describe the excitement they felt on seeing Hitler in person in 1931. So emotionally stirred that they could not sleep, they stayed up all night talking about the wondrous Führer who was everything they had longed for. Together they prayed that nothing would harm him or remove him from them; together they asked forgiveness for ever doubting him as their Führer. They joined the Party and volunteered for service to help feed and care for Nazi Storm Troopers.

## A CHILDISH NATURE

In reflecting on the amazing success of Adolf Hitler, an American psychiatrist wondered why Germans followed this particular leader who was essentially so *childish;* what was it in them, he asked, that responded to this immature person who was in so many ways ridiculous? It seems likely that the Youth Cohort felt drawn to Hitler precisely *because* he was childlike and exhibited traits so similar to their own. He too used the defense of regression; he too, they believed, had suffered hunger and deprivation; he too was filled with hatred and capable of furious temper tantrums. Like themselves, he was defensive and vulnerable, but he could also be brutal and dictatorial in his demands, a destroyer and creator who would repay the insult of Versailles and build a New Order. He, too, practiced "primitive idealization": the world was divided into the All Good and the All Evil—the good, creative Aryans, the evil, destructive Jews.

Above all, the Youth Cohort came to Hitler because his movement institutionalized hatred and sanctified aggression. It was exactly what the Cohort needed to cope with the rage and frustration that had been experienced during their infancy and reinforced in late adolescence, during the Depression. The sheer violence of Hitler's movement served to redirect feelings of hostility. For the father-Führer was not merely a replacement for the distant and idealized father. He also served as a psychological defense against the destructive resentment they still felt toward their fathers who had deserted them. In short, the psychological problems of the Youth Cohort gave Hitler a unique opportunity to project upon the German masses the same unconscious conflicts that had shaped his own infancy. In this instance, as in many others, "his own pathology harmonized with that of Germany," as Andreas Dorpalen writes.

## YOUTHFUL ANTI-SEMITISM

Hitler's hatred of the Jews was another major attraction for the young people of Germany. For his racist ideology spoke directly to their own prejudices. Anti-Semitism was one of the striking features of the Weimar youth movement, as it was of the Free Corps and of university life. Almost all the dueling fraternities, for example, contained "Aryan clauses" in their charters, as did the largest Catholic association of university students.

Martin Wangh, an American psychiatrist who has investigated the psychological origins of the genocide of the Jews, has found roots in the Nazi Youth Cohort's infantile experience during World War I. He believes that as young boys during the war, they discovered that their Oedipal longings increased during the father's long absence. Since strong incestuous desires for the mother could not be tolerated, they were projected and blamed on someone else. The psychological defense used was the same as the one employed by young Adolf Hitler: they, too, ascribed incest to the Jews, who sought the ruination of the German people. The Jews were the racial enemy who should be punished and removed as "incestuous criminals" and "defilers of the race." Thus, exactly as with Hitler, "self-contempt was displaced onto the Jews . . . thereby assuaging feelings of unworthiness and masochistic fantasies of rejection." According to Dr. Wangh, such fantasies of self-destruction led to a more ominous displacement when feelings of suicidal depression were transformed into a program of mass murder.

It is probably true that anti-Semitism was less important in Hitler's accession to power than the economic crisis of 1930–1933. Nevertheless, the economic and social distress of those years served to reinforce already existent anti-Semitism, particularly among the Youth Cohort. For hatred of the Jews was a very effective way of bringing together primitive urges to hate, attack, and destroy. Hitler's anti-Semitism also appealed to the Cohort because it provided a way to lessen guilt feelings for having abandoned traditional Christian teachings. As psychoanalyst Erik Erikson has reminded us, young people seek some sort of faith and commitment. In this era of national humiliation, resentment, and the Versailles Treaty, thousands of young Germans found Christianity irrelevant to their needs. They wanted hatred and revenge, not love and reconciliation. But they still felt uneasy about rejecting the religion of their childhood. To such people, as Maurice Samuel has suggested in *The Great Hatred,* anti-Semitism was a kind of displaced hatred of Christianity, a way of decreasing guilt feelings by attacking the traditional enemy of Christianity, the Jew. Thus the emphasis of the Oberammergau passion plays of the period: hate the Jews, for the Jews killed Jesus. Hitler's anti-Semitism provided "the official rehabilitation of hatred," in the words of Eva G. Reichmann.

There was a need to hate, and Hitler supplied it. But it is a mistake to see his appeal solely in negative terms. Rather, he was effective because he spoke *both* to the basest and to the most lofty impulses of man: to hatred, cruelty, aggression, and terror, but also to faith, hope, love, and sacrifice. One of the reasons why Hitler was such an effective leader was that he thoroughly understood a profound psychological truth: neither a man nor a political party lives by bread alone. Both need sustaining ideals. Political programs are never successful if they cast their appeals solely in terms of materialism, self-interest, and cupidity. Hitler's Youth Cohort wanted very much to believe that their leader could inspire them with ideals of service, sacrifice, and patriotism.

## A MESSAGE OF HOPE

Hitler, an opportunist but also man of faith, found it easy to put on the armor of righteousness: he would save Germany from selfishness, materialism, factionalism, moral depravity, racial corruption. The effectiveness of his propaganda lay finally in this—he made it seem that his party's nihilism was idealism, its brutality strength, its vicious "ideology" altruism. And his converts in the name of idealism were legion. Historian H.R. Trevor-Roper is right in reminding us that not all adherents of Hitler were vicious anti-Semites, sadistic brutes, bullies, and neurotics. "Many young people," he has written, "bewildered by the confusion of their time, were inspired by the message of hope, the simple, crystal-clear, infectious insurance" that a nation defeated and bound could, by the exercise of faith and willpower, arise again to a position of pride and independence.

The memoirs of hundreds of young people who gladly joined Hitler's movement speak eloquently of such hope and idealism. Young people were particularly attracted by the promise of a *Gemeinschaft* [community] where common good would come before personal interest, where brotherly concern and support of an inspired leader would solve the problems of Germany and end the awful feelings of individual isolation and individual responsibility. Many who were incensed by national defeat and the dishonor of Versailles might normally have supported traditional nationalist parties. But such parties as the Conservatives and the German National People's Party had nothing to offer this Youth Cohort, who believed that the conservative groups merely talked about patriotism while seeking to restore caste privilege. The idealistic young people wanted a united cooperative community, not the old social order. They found what they sought in Hitler. A student wrote:

> How different from [traditional party politics] was the daring
> proposition that sprang from Hitler's warm, sympathetic
> heart! His idea was not to use the resources of the State to
> help industrialists and landowners, but to take advantage of
> them immediately to relieve the misery of millions of unem-
> ployed Germans!

A young laborer was attracted to Hitler because he believed that Hitler shared his desire for sacrifice and his faith
in the Fatherland: "Faith was the one thing that always led
us on, faith in Germany, faith in the purity of our nation and
faith in our Leader." The memoir of a young soldier strikes
the same note of faith and sacrifice: "It is superfluous to describe the sacrifices I made. . . . [They] were made in the
spirit of *Gemeinsshaft*."

# Hitler Deceived the Germans

Eberhard Jäckel

Historian Eberhard Jäckel teaches at the University of Stuttgart in Germany and has written prolifically on Adolf Hitler, mostly in German. The following piece is excerpted from his book *Hitler in History.* Jäckel asserts that Hitler did not truly care about the German people and betrayed their love for him. The Germans so admired Hitler, Jäckel says, that they refused to believe he was involved in—or even knew about—many of the atrocities carried out by the Nazis. In fact, he reveals, the Germans often felt that if Hitler could only be informed about these horrors, he would stop them. According to the author, Hitler deliberately deceived the German people about his intentions in order to win their trust, and the Germans responded by deceiving themselves about Hitler's true nature.

Only rarely did Hitler and the Germans call each other by their proper names while they were contemporaries and made history together. Hitler usually did not address them as Germans, but as German folk comrades, and when he referred to them, he preferred to use the collective form and spoke of the German people or the German. He would say, for instance, that a German youth must be "as tough as leather and as hard as Krupp steel." Or that "for the German soldier nothing is impossible." The Germans, for their part, almost without exception called him the führer (even though they greeted each other with the phrase "Heil Hitler"), and the prescribed form of address was "my führer." The more intimate appellations applied to many statesmen were not at all commonly used, and it would have been unthinkable for a cheering crowd to shout "Adolf."

Excerpted from *Hitler in History*, by Eberhard Jäckel, pp. 88–91 (Boston: Brandeis University Press). Copyright ©1984 by Eberhard Jäckel. Reprinted by permission of University Press of New England.

This seems to point to a rather impersonal relationship. But regardless of whether Hitler and the Germans loved each other or feared each other, what they thought of each other and, above all, how the one could emerge from the other are questions that can find their answers in a historical analysis.

## No Love Lost

Hitler always kept in mind what he had written in his book *Mein Kampf*: "The basic foundation for establishing authority is always popularity." He immediately qualified that sentence and saw "in power . . . in force" the other principal basis of all authority. Nevertheless, no saying of his has been handed down to posterity that even remotely resembles the words engraved on Napoleon's tomb: "May my ashes rest on the banks of the Seine near the people whom I loved so dearly." That Hitler loved the Germans is a dubious proposition; indeed he did not even want to be buried on the Spree, but in Linz on the Danube [in Austria].

Just as Alexander the Great was not a Greek, Napoleon not a Frenchman, and Stalin not a Russian, so Hitler came from the outside, at the least from outside the boundaries of the German national state created by Otto von Bismarck, and he spoke of the Germans in a distant manner, as if he didn't really belong to them. "Here too I am as cold as ice," he remarked during the war. "If the German people are not prepared to do battle for their self-preservation, then fine, let them perish!" Even in public speeches he made these comments, as on December 18, 1940, to a group of officer candidates: "This nation will fade away" if it fails to assert its claim to existence. Then "it should vanish," he declared to a foreign statesman on November 27, 1941. Moreover he would "not shed a tear for it." To be sure he wanted to make Germany great, greater than it had ever been in history. But he was less concerned with Germans as individuals—with their well-being and their fortunes—than with German blood, which he shed coldheartedly in order to expand the nation.

## Hitler's Spell on the Germans

The Germans, by contrast, loved him rather than feared him. . . . Under Hitler the Germans never doubted, despaired, or revolted as they might have under a tyrant. Forces from abroad had to take him away from them, and only then was the spell that had bound them to each other for over twelve years broken, and it was broken immediately. Perhaps nothing characterizes the relationship of the Germans to Hitler so aptly as a phrase that was making the rounds in those days and went like this: "If only the führer knew about that!" Being applicable and indeed applied to the petty nuisances of daily life as well as to the great horrors of the regime, it absolved the führer (who after all could not concern himself with everything) of responsibility for specific events and also elevated him to the ranks of the unimpeachable.

One example can serve as evidence. When the mentally ill were being put to death by the tens of thousands at the beginning of the war, the district leader of a Nazi women's organization (certainly no enemy of the regime) wrote to the wife of the chief justice of the Nazi party on November 25, 1940: "People are still clinging to the hope that the führer knows nothing about these things, that he can't possibly know, otherwise he would stop them." And again, "The matter must be brought to the attention of the führer before it is too late and there must be a way for the voice of the German people to reach the ear of its führer." A twofold deception! Naturally, Hitler knew what was to be brought to his attention. After all, it issued from his mouth and figured as his command. But far more important, the horrified reaction of the people not only reached him; he even listened to it, rescinded the order, and ended the operation.

## Two Types of Deception

In general, the relationship of the Germans to Hitler rested on deception, conscious deception on his part and self-deception on their part. He concealed his plans from them, although he knew exactly what he wanted, and they failed to recognize in him a causal agent even when he translated his intentions into action. They rewarded his deception with trust and, even under the worst circumstances, did not believe that they were being deceived but rather that he was being deceived.

## CHAPTER 3

# Hitler, World War II, and the Holocaust

# Hitler's War Aims

H.R. Trevor-Roper

Now retired, H.R. Trevor-Roper formerly held the prestigious position of Regius Professor of Modern History at Oxford University in England. Shortly after the end of the Second World War, he served as part of a British intelligence group that investigated the circumstances of Hitler's death—an experience he drew on for his book *The Last Days of Hitler*. In the following essay, Trevor-Roper asserts that Adolf Hitler had consistent war aims, which he expressed as early as 1924 in *Mein Kampf*. Foremost among these goals was the conquest of Russia, which Hitler planned to make into a German colony, according to Trevor-Roper. He maintains that although Hitler sometimes modified his plans temporarily (as in 1939, when Germany and Russia became allies), he never lost sight of his primary goals and always worked toward achieving them. Trevor-Roper also notes that Hitler's attempt to conquer Russia proved to be the cause of Germany's undoing in the war.

Adolf Hitler's war aims are written large and clear in the documents of his reign. They are quite different from the war aims of the men who, in 1933, admitted him to power and who, after 1933, served him in power. They are also, in my opinion, different from the aims which have sometimes been ascribed to him by historians who regard him as a mere power-loving opportunist. In this essay I wish to show these differences. I shall do so with the aid of four personal sources. Other more casual documents could easily be used to confirm these sources, but for the present I will be content with these four.

## FOUR IMPORTANT DOCUMENTS

These four sources to which I refer are, first, *Mein Kampf*, Hitler's personal credo, written in prison in 1924 after the

Excerpted from "Hitler's War Aims," by H.R. Trevor-Roper, ©1985 H.R. Trevor-Roper, in *Aspects of the Third Reich*, edited by H.W. Koch. Reprinted with permission of St. Martin's Press, Inc.

total collapse of his first bid for power; secondly, Hermann Rauschning's *Gespräche mit Hitler* [Talks with Hitler], which were first published in 1939 and are the record of Hitler's private political conversations at the time of his second and successful bid, that is, in 1932–4; thirdly, the official record of Hitler's *Tischgespräche* [Table Talks], at the time of his apparently universal military triumph in 1941–2; and, finally, the similar record of his *Tischgespräche* at the time when he first acknowledged final defeat, in February 1945. These four documents are like four windows, opened, by different hands, into the inmost recesses of Hitler's mind at four crucial moments of his career: the moments of political defeat, political triumph, military triumph, military defeat. The first window was flung wide open by himself: it was his challenge to the world to show that he did not accept the defeat of 1918. The second he would no doubt have preferred to keep shut: in 1932–34 he had no wish to publish his radical programme before he had built up the political and military base that was to sustain it; it was an enemy's, or rather a traitor's hand which opened it. The last two windows were opened by Hitler himself, but privately. The world was intended to look in, but not yet. Posterity, not the present generation, was to see the secret of his triumph, the cause of his defeat.

Now the interesting thing about all these documents is that though spread over a period of 22 years, and issued in these very different circumstances, they all show an absolute consistency of philosophy and purpose. This consistency, this purpose has often been denied. It was denied at the time by those, in Germany and abroad, who wished to disbelieve it: whether, like some western statesmen, they feared to contemplate this hideous new power or, like some German statesmen, they hoped to harness it to their own more limited aims; and it has been denied since, by historians who are so revolted by Hitler's personal character, by the vulgarity and cruelty of his mind, that they refuse to allow him such virtues as mental power and consistency. But in fact I believe that all these denials are wrong. The statesmen were proved wrong by events. The historians, in my opinion (though they include some distinguished names among my own compatriots—Sir Lewis Namier, Alan Bullock, A.J.P. Taylor) err by confusing moral with intellectual judgments. That Hitler's mind was vulgar and cruel I readily agree; but vulgarity and cruelty are not inconsistent with power and consistency.

## MEIN KAMPF

Let us take first the evidence of *Mein Kampf*, once the most widely distributed though by no means the most widely read book after the Bible. The dreadful jargon in which *Mein Kampf* is written, its hysterical tone and shameless propaganda, should not blind us to the crude but real mental power which underlies it. The book is the expression of a political philosophy fully formed. In it Hitler declares himself to be a student of history convinced by his studies that a new age of history is now about to begin. He also declares clearly what kind of an age this will be. The age of small, maritime powers ruling the world through sea-communications, seapower and the wealth built up by overseas colonisation, he says, is now closing. With them, the whole world that they have created must gradually dissolve. Instead of distant overseas colonies, which have become useless, power will now depend on great land-masses such as modern techniques can now at last mobilise. Moreover, thanks to those same techniques, whatever power succeeds in mobilising such land-masses can base upon them a lasting empire. The only question is, what power can mobilise them first? When he asks himself this question, Hitler obviously has in mind only two powers, Germany and Russia. In 1923 both Germany and Russia were defeated powers. Was it conceivable that either of them could rise from such defeat to seize this unique historical opportunity?

To an outsider, without faith, it might well seem that neither Germany nor Russia was equipped for such a task. But Hitler had faith. He believed that Germany could do it. Not Weimar Germany of course, defeated, demoralised, disarmed. Nor even monarchist Germany: the monarchy was too weak. It has had its chance and failed. History has condemned it. Moreover, it is also too conservative. The monarchists aim only at restoration, the restoration of the frontiers of 1914, the colonies of 1914. But the frontiers of 1914, says Hitler, are anachronistic in the new age, and so are the colonies: such an ambition is, to him, meaningless and contemptible. 'Monarchies', he would say later, 'serve to keep empires; only revolutions can conquer them.' And so, in 1923, Hitler advocated a revolution: not a mere palace revolution, but a historic revolution, comparable with the Russian revolution: a revolution which would release a new historic force. Moreover, Hitler made it perfectly clear that he was himself the demiurge of such a revolution. He was, he said, one of those world-phenomena which occur only at rare intervals in time, at once philosophers able to understand and practical politicians able to exploit the turning-points of world history. If only he could obtain power, Hitler wrote in 1924, he would create, out of German nationalism, now red and raw with defeat, a revolutionary force which would resume the historic mission of Germany and conquer, not distant colonies, the chimera of Wilhelmine [monarchist] Germany, but, from infamous Bolshevik [communist] Russia, the vast land-spaces of the East. . . .

## IGNORING HITLER'S WARNINGS

The importance of *Mein Kampf* as a real declaration of Hitler's considered and practical war aims, even in 1924, is often overlooked. But it is shown by one small fact among many. Although every German was enabled and expected to read it, Hitler consistently used his copyright to prevent any full translation, at least into English. The authorised English edition was a miserable abridgement, one-fifth of the full length, and it was not until 1939 that an English publisher broke the ban and published a pirated translation. And so English (and other) politicians and political writers consistently ignored the plain statements in *Mein Kampf*, or wishfully maintained either that Hitler did not mean what he said, or that he could not do what he meant. One notable exception was the distinguished English historian and publicist, the late Sir Robert Ensor. After 1933 Ensor consistently maintained that Hitler would make war, and in 1936 he declared roundly that he would annex Austria in the spring of 1938 and either cause a European war or a European surrender to avoid war over Czechoslovakia in the autumn of 1938. When his predictions were verified and he was asked to give his reasons, Ensor gave them: their starting-point was, 'I had the advantage—still too rare in England and then only just not unique—of having read *Mein Kampf* in the German'. I particularly remember this incident, because it was thanks to it that I also mustered the energy to read through the turgid pages of that barbarous, but important work.

If men would not take *Mein Kampf*, which Hitler himself

had written, seriously, they would hardly pay much regard to Rauschning's revelations, whose authenticity could not be proved. Indeed, I am told that, when they were published in 1939, British prime minister Neville Chamberlain, obstinate in his illusions, declared that he simply didn't believe a word of it, but to anyone who has read *Mein Kampf,* Rauschning's revelation of Hitler's vast ambitions of world conquest has few surprises. Perhaps the most interesting thing about Rauschning's book is its date: the date both of its contents and of its publication. Its contents, being of 1932–4, show that the passage of ten years and the acquisition of power and its responsibilities had not reduced Hitler's vast and revolutionary aims in the least. The date of publication, 1939, shows that Rauschning was equally faithful in recording the expression of those aims. For in 1939 Hitler had made a pact with Russia in order to make war on Poland and the West. Many people in the West and in Germany accepted this pact as evidence that Hitler was now committed to the old programme. If Rauschning had really (as was said) merely written a topical work, he would hardly have included one passage, which then seemed false but which history has since shown to be true—but in fact he did include it. It is the passage in which Hitler, having repudiated the acquisition of colonies and disdained the pre-war frontiers of Germany, went on to speak of Russia. 'Perhaps I shall not be able to avoid an alliance with Russia' he said. 'I shall keep that as a trump-card. Perhaps it will be the decisive gamble of my life. . . . But it will never stop me from as firmly retracing my steps and attacking Russia when my aims in the west have been achieved. . . . We alone can conquer the great continental space, and it will be done by us singly and alone, not through a pact with Moscow. We shall take this struggle upon us. It will open to us the door to permanent mastery of the world.'

## CONSISTENT WAR AIMS?

Thus from 1920 to 1939 Hitler's aims were clear: repudiation of colonies, repudiation of the old imperial frontiers (those, he said, were an ambition 'unworthy of our revolution'), and instead the creation of a revolutionary, nationalist force able to conquer permanently 'the great continental space' of Russia. In the face of this reiterated clarity, it seems odd to me that distinguished historians should insist that Hitler had no such consistent war aims: that F.H. Hinsley, for instance, in his work on *Hitler's Strategy*, should argue that Hitler only made war on Russia in 1941 in order to acquire the means of breaking the obstinacy of Britain, and that A.J.P. Taylor, reluctant to allow Hitler any consistency, should maintain that he had a series of interchangeable philosophies—i.e. convenient theories—which he would produce at will, as occasion required. . . . But since these historians use these arguments, let me answer them.

Of course it is true that, at different times, Hitler was prepared to say almost anything, and we can never believe anything to be true *merely* because he said it. However, since some of his statements of aims must have been true, even if at other times contradicted by him, we cannot reject everything out of hand: we must find a criterion of veracity. Now I believe that such a criterion is easily found. Hitler's statements of his aims can be accepted as true provided they are explicable not merely by immediate tactical necessity but, first, as part of a general philosophy regularly expressed even in adverse tactical circumstances, and secondly by long-term practical preparations. Once we apply these tests, Hitler's alternative 'philosophies' soon dissolve: only the philosophy of an eastern empire remains. If Hitler raged at France in 1923, that was merely because France was then the centre of a system of eastern alliances. . . . In 1941, when he had to explain away to an outraged Benito Mussolini [the Italian dictator] or a dismayed German naval command his sudden war on Russia, he naturally explained to them that this was really the best way of winning their war against England. However, Mussolini on 3 January 1940, in a letter to Hitler, had asked him not to 'betray his revolution' but destroy Bolshevism and secure living space in Russia. Hitler took two months until he wrote a negative reply. But in fact his practical preparations, his systematic policy, show that he was not interested in either England or France: his real war was, as he so consistently stated, not a conservative war against the West but a revolutionary war against Russia.

## HITLER'S GREAT DECEPTION

In this matter of his real aims it was not only foreigners and historians whom Hitler deceived. He also deceived what for convenience I shall call the German Establishment. By this term I mean the German conservative civil servants and generals and politicians who, in 1933, brought him to power and who, from 1933 onwards, at least for a time, served him faithfully, only to be bitterly disillusioned and sometimes, from dupes, to become martyrs. . . . These men, I have already suggested, had war aims: or rather, political aims which might have to be realised by war, though they hoped to achieve them peacefully. They wanted, naturally, to restore German pride, shattered by defeat. They wanted to restore the army as an essential institution of state. They wanted to recover lost territory. But their territorial aims were limited: they did not want to swallow again the indigestible morsel of Alsace-Lorraine. What they wanted was land in the East only—but old lands, not new. They wanted the old imperial frontiers in Poland. If they were prepared to go a little further than the Kaiser and absorb Austria and the Sudetenland also, that was rather a necessity imposed by the collapse [of the old empire] than a sign of political ambitions in south-east Europe. For the demands of these men were essentially limited, essentially conservative. They might hate Russia for its Bolshevism, but they had no desire to conquer it. A war of conquest against Russia, quite apart from the cost and the risks, would entail (as Hitler himself said, it would necessitate) a German revolution. A German revolution was not wanted by the German Establishment. How then, we may ask, could the German Establishment be so mistaken as to give themselves, as indispensable agents of his policy, to a man who was not only so criminal in his methods but also so completely opposed to them in his aims?

The reasons, of course, are many. There was weakness, there was self-deception, there was subtle bribery. In many ways the German Establishment was not an establishment: it was not an aristocracy, rooted in tradition or bound together by common principles: it was a caste, an interest-group, rotted within; and Hitler exploited the rot. But also there was a hard fact of geography. One has only to look at the map of Europe to see that in order to carry out his large policy, Hitler had to begin by carrying out their small policy. Their policy was to increase German respect and self-respect by the possession of an army, in which also they were professionally interested; to knock France out of eastern Europe; and then to recover the old eastern frontiers at the expense of Poland and incorporate the Austro-Germans and the Sudeten Germans in the Reich. Then they wanted to stop. For such limited aims Hitler of course had, and expressed, nothing but contempt. He wanted to conquer Russia and occupy it permanently, up to the Urals, perhaps beyond. But how could he reach Russia except through Poland, or Poland except by detaching France? For sheer geographical reasons Hitler had to begin his revolutionary policy by carrying out the conservative policy of the Establishment. This was very convenient to him. It enabled him, by playing down his ulterior aims for the time being, to buy their support. Then, when he had carried out their policy for them, he could afford to come out into the open. He was armed, victorious, unstoppable. He went on to realise his own. The full achievement of their aims was merely the essential preliminary for the achievement of his. . . .

## FOCUS ON RUSSIA

So Hitler set out in 1941 to realise his permanent war aims. Leaving the irrelevant West to its impotent, meaningless resistance, he turned east to conquer, in one brief campaign, the prize of history. After the war there were many who said that Hitler's Russian campaign was his greatest 'mistake'. If only he had kept peace with Russia, they said, he could have absorbed, organised and fortified Europe, and Britain would never have been able to dislodge him. But this view, in my opinion, rests on a fallacy: it assumes that Hitler was not Hitler. To Hitler the Russian campaign was not a luxury, an extra campaign, a diversion in search of supplies or the expedient of temporary frustration: it was the be-all and end-all of Nazism. Not only could it not be omitted: it could not even be delayed. It was now or never that this great epochal battle must be fought. . . . So urgent was it that Hitler could not even wait for victory in the West. That, he said, could be won afterwards: when Russia was conquered, even English obstinacy would give in: meanwhile he must strike, and strike quickly in the East.

Why was Hitler in such a hurry? Because, he believed, time was against him. If he waited, there was the added cost of the huge armed forces which he had created, the danger that their weapons would become obsolete while he waited, the fact that the Nazi leaders were ageing, the German birthrate declining, the fear that 'some idiot with a bomb' might assassinate the only man strong enough to carry through that 'Cyclopean task', the building of an empire. On the other hand the Russian population was increasing, Russian industry was expanding, and in ten or fifteen years Russia would be 'the mightiest state in the world'. Therefore, Hitler had said in 1937 'it is certain that we can wait no longer. . . . If the Führer is still living, then it will be his irrevocable decision to solve the German space problem no later than 1943–5. . . . After that date we can only expect a change for the worse.' If Hitler had merely contemplated war against the 'decaying' West, there was no hurry. It was the eastern war in which time, even history, was against him: history which by haste and willpower he hoped to reverse. He would reverse it by rolling back, at the last possible minute, the Asiatic barbarians from 'the Heartland'. . . .

'The Heartland' was East Europe and European Russia. Hitler saw himself and Russian leader Joseph Stalin as two giants competing, with revolutionary force, for control of this Heartland; and he knew that whichever of them won was ruthless enough to make his conquest permanent. The politicians of the Establishment could have no such ambitions because, apart from anything else, they were too mild. . . . They thought in terms of conventional wars, wars for power. Hitler might fight such a conventional war in the West, and therefore in the West he would respect the old conventions of war; but this eastern war was quite different: it was a war for the wholesale possession of land and the right to clear off, or reduce to abject slavery, the former inhabitants of the land. Conventions would be ignored; quarter would be neither given nor asked; Moscow itself would be razed to the ground, and its name and memory blotted out from history and geography alike.

## HITLER'S IMPERIAL GOALS

In 1941, when Hitler had launched his final war, and felt the crunch of victory on all fronts, he thought that his great hour had come. Now at last the consistent aim of twenty years was about to be fulfilled. Therefore, he judged, it was time, once again, to declare his testament, to open another window into his mind. And so his faithful high-priest and secretary, Martin Bormann, made all the arrangements. At his headquarters, in East Prussia or in the Ukraine, Hitler sat and talked, and obedient stenographers, placed behind screens, took down the holy writ: Hitler's *Tischgespräche*, or rather his monologues, on the power he had achieved and the empire he was now at last about to create.

Hitler's *Tischgespräche* is a dreadful document, repellent and yet fascinating, the multiple mirror of a mind completely empty of humanity and yet charged with fierce, systematising, sometimes clarifying power. 'I have the gift', Hitler once said 'of reducing all problems to their simplest form': and here he reduced them. Sometimes the simplicity is terrifying. . . ; but at least it is always clear; and nothing is more clear than his picture of the New Order now about to be established in the East; a nightmare, barbarian empire, without humanity, without culture, without purpose, 'a new Dark Age', as Sir Winston Churchill once described the consequences of a Nazi victory, 'made more sinister, and perhaps more protracted, by the lights of perverted science'. For the sole purpose of empire, Hitler declared, was to sustain itself, to minister to national pride. 'Who has, has': that is the sum of political morality; and the greatest folly that a master-race can commit is to give anything up or so to arm its subjects that they may enforce a claim to freedom. Therefore, in the new German empire, subject peoples must possess no arms; they must acquire no education (except the knowledge of enough German to obey orders); and they must be taught contraception and denied hospitals in order that both dwindling births and unhampered death may keep their numbers down. Thus reduced, the enslaved Russians can live on as a depressed Helot [slave] class, hewing wood and drawing water for a privileged aristocracy of German colonists who will sit securely in fortified cities, connected by strategic autobahns [highways], glorying in their nationality and listening to *The Merry Widow* for ever and ever. For 'after National Socialism has lasted for some time, it will be impossible even to imagine a form of life different from ours.'

Such was Hitler's ultimate millenium. In 1941 he thought he had realised it. In February 1945 the hope of it had gone, apparently for ever, and even Hitler was forced to admit it. It was a desperate admission, and he had long refused to make it, but now there was no evading it, and the only question was, how had such a disastrous reversal of fortune come about? How indeed? As Hitler reflected on it, he decided that once again it was his duty to enlighten posterity by opening a window into his mind. So in Berlin, the machinery was mounted, the screen set, the stenographer placed, and Hitler opened the fourth window into the working of his mind, the last chapter of his holy writ: his explanation of defeat.

## EXPLAINING DEFEAT

And how did he explain it? Did he ever suggest, as so many others have suggested, that he was wrong to have made war on Russia, that he should have stopped, as the German Establishment would have liked to stop, in 1940? Certainly not. Admittedly, he allows, a useful peace could have been made with England in 1940 or 1941, with advantage to both sides: for both had gained victories over their degenerate Latin enemies—Germany over France, England over Italy. But Hitler was quick to add that this peace would have been merely tactical not final: its purpose would have been not a final settlement but the redirection of Germany's war effort. 'Germany, secure in her rear, could then have thrown herself, heart and soul, into her real task, the mission of my life, the *raison d'être* [reason for existence] of National Socialism: the destruction of Bolshevism'. 'It is eastwards, only and always eastwards, that the veins of our life must expand.'

How then did Hitler explain his disastrous failure? In these last conversations he goes through many possibilities. Was it in going to war at all? That suggestion is made only to be dismissed: from the very beginning the whole purpose of Nazism was war. Was it then in launching his war too soon? No, he would not admit that. Russia had to be attacked: a dozen reasons demanded haste. In fact, he now maintained, it would have been far better if he had begun earlier, if he had launched his essential preliminary war against the West in 1938 instead of 1939. But alas, at that time Germany, though materially armed, was morally unprepared, encumbered with reactionary generals and diplomats. . . .

## BLAMING MUSSOLINI

What then could the hitch be? In the end, after long fumbling, Hitler found it. It was his trust in Mussolini, he decided, which had ruined him. Of course he greatly admired Mussolini, he owed much to his example, much to his friendship, . . . but in 1941 Mussolini had been a disastrous ally. By his misadventures in the Mediterranean, and particularly by his ill-timed and unannounced adventure in Greece, Mussolini had dragged Hitler into the Balkans to rescue him, and had forced him, by that diversion, to delay by five weeks his attack on Russia. For the attack on Russia had been planned for 15 May: in fact, owing to the demands of the Balkan campaign, it was not launched until 22 June.

And what was the result? To Hitler, at least in retrospect, it was clear, his Russian campaign had been designed as a *Blitzkrieg*: it was to be over in one summer; and if he had only had one full summer, it would have been. But he had started late, five weeks late, and then the winter, that terrible Russian winter, had come unexpectedly early: and so the armies had been snowed up, the programme halted, the Russians had had time to recover, the English to plot new alliances, new campaigns in the rear. . . . When Hitler looked back and thought how nearly he had won everything that he had ever sought in 1941, and how his triumph had dissolved even as he was celebrating it, he could almost weep with chagrin. 'That idiotic campaign in Greece!' he would exclaim, 'If the war had remained a war conducted by Germany and not by the Axis, we should have been in a position to attack Russia by 15 May, 1941. Doubly fortified by the fact that our forces had known nothing but decisive and irrefutable victory, we should have been able to conclude the campaign before winter came. How differently everything has turned out!'

Thus to the end Hitler maintained the purity of his war aims. To him, from 1920 to 1945, the purpose of Nazism was always the same: it was to create an empire, to wrest the 'great continental space' of Russia from the Russians. Even after defeat he did not seek to cloak it. A month after issuing this last testament, he told Nazi architect Albert Speer that Germany had failed him and deserved to perish: 'the future belongs solely to the stronger Eastern nation'. And the day before his death, the last words of his last message sent out of the Bunker in Berlin to the Wehrmacht [the German army] was an adjuration that 'the aim must still be to win territory in the East for the German people'.

## ONE CLEAR AMBITION

Thus Hitler's ultimate strategic aims can be detached with absolute clarity, absolute consistency, from the tactical necessities or concessions which surround them. At different times he was under different necessities and made different concessions. In 1923 France, in 1940 England stood between him and his goal. But these were not his real enemies.

France, once conquered and rendered harmless, was let alone, even pampered: the British on landing in Normandy were astonished at the plenty they found there. . . . Similarly, inside Germany, the Establishment, the old conservative classes, with their limited aims, stood between him and his policy. Hitler's tactics took account of these obstacles. Throughout the 1930s, although *Mein Kampf* sat in every bookcase, its doctrines were muted, at least in public and abroad, and Hitler was quite content that they should be written off as juvenile indiscretions. In 1939, he would make 'the greatest gamble in his life': the Russo-German Pact. But all these were tactical necessities. In private Hitler never ceased to utter the doctrines of *Mein Kampf.* And in 1941, when France, England and the German Establishment were all defeated, he threw off the mask. The original authentic voice rang out again. He set out, over the corpses of enemies and accomplices alike, to achieve 'the ambition of my life, the *raison d'être* of National Socialism'—the conquest of the East.

# Hitler Underestimated the United States

James V. Compton

Most historians agree that Hitler did not intend to provoke a war with the United States while he was occupied with his military campaign against Russia. Germany declared war on the United States only because of its pact with Japan: After Japan bombed Pearl Harbor in December 1941 and America responded by declaring war on the Japanese, Germany was required by the pact to support Japan. This turn of events was decisive in determining the outcome of the Second World War, since the addition of the U.S. military into the European conflict ensured Germany's eventual defeat. In the following article, taken from his book *The Swastika and the Eagle: Hitler, the United States, and the Origins of World War II*, James V. Compton explains that Hitler had consistently underestimated the likelihood that America would enter the war. He writes that most of Germany's diplomats in Washington, D.C., and other Nazi officials who traveled frequently in the United States warned Hitler of the strong anti-German sentiment in the country. However, Hitler ignored their reports and neglected to plan military strategies for dealing with a potential attack from the United States, Compton concludes. Compton is a history professor at San Francisco State University.

In one stroke the Japanese attack on Pearl Harbor on December 7, 1941, converted the European conflict into a war of universal dimensions. With the German declaration of war upon the United States four days later German-American tensions became part of the wider military struggles of the Second World War. U.S. president Franklin Roo-

Excerpted from *The Swastika and the Eagle: Hitler, the United States, and the Origins of World War II*, by James V. Compton. Copyright ©1967 by James V. Compton. Reprinted by permission of David Higham Associates as agents for the author.

sevelt and Adolf Hitler at last stood opposed to one another on the battlefield. This belligerency was ironic, for Hitler had not intended it and never fully realized its implications, yet he contributed enormously to it. In the pattern of events preceding the outbreak of hostilities, we see clearly revealed some of the general defects, limitations and paradoxes of his politics and strategy.

## HITLER'S OPINION OF AMERICA

The Fuehrer was prepared to reject America out of hand because of his requirements for national greatness, his proposed solution of the German question and the limitations of his strategic world. National power, based upon blood, individual genius and the will to survive, required the authoritarian state and not liberal democracy which was always fraudulent and anti-racial. Germany's problems could not be met through colonial or economic solutions but only through the acquisition of contiguous *Lebensraum* [living space] in the East. Finally, Hitler's world was, at least as he described it, primarily Central European and did not seem to involve non-European areas in any immediate way, although intensive conquest might well have become extensive had he secured his European base.

Hitler's spoken and written comments on America were vague and ill-informed. He relied here on random unofficial and party sources whose information was then passed through a clutter of prejudices, emerging for the most part as invective to be used on suitable occasions. He listened to Nazi fundraiser Kurt Ludecke, Nazi member Ernest "Putzi" Hanfstaengl, German travel writer Colin Ross and others with obvious impatience, selecting what was useful to him. Little about this country could have been appetizing. Capitalist materialism, the large Jewish element, the free press, the democratic idealism of Franklin Roosevelt to say nothing of the distance from Europe and the maritime factors involved violated almost every rule of national greatness and most of the criteria for admission to Hitler's world. He scarcely bothered to conceal his contempt. The country was decadent, Roosevelt the enemy of civilization. Unwilling to face the importance of the American role in the first war and using former U.S. president Woodrow Wilson as a scapegoat for the German defeat, he convinced himself that the internal condition and external position of the United States rendered an American role in Europe out of the question. A picture of isolation, military weakness, social division, economic distress and racial decay now allowed Hitler to tend to more congenial continental problems. Toward American aid to Germany's enemies and even a possible entry into the war, he professed the most complete indifference.

## THE VIEW OF GERMANY'S DIPLOMATS

For his diplomats, whom he distrusted but could not dispense with, America had always been an important factor and they accorded that country a considerable role in their reports and recommendations. Those concerned with American affairs in Berlin as well as the chiefs of the German embassy in Washington, D.C., were in general balanced and realistic in their approach. Without illusions concerning American hostility to German domestic and foreign policy, they presented a picture in Berlin quite at variance with what Hitler chose to believe. Economic power, potential military strength, national unity and a determined and popular leadership were the features of American life which most impressed the diplomats. As these features could by definition not be those of a capitalist democracy and racial melting pot, they were not entertained at the Reichschancellory.

In foreign policy, the isolationism upon which Hitler relied as the only possible stance for a country so lacking in national virtue was waved aside (perhaps too lightly) in the dispatches as a temporary thing already seriously weakened by the vigorous reaction to German aggression. Berlin was repeatedly warned that America would not sit idly by and see England defeated; that economic aid would be forthcoming and military assistance not impossible; that Americans were convinced of a world conspiracy of aggression which was bound to affect their hemisphere; that in 1940 and 1941 American policy was moving boldly from neutrality to a *de facto* participation in the war. Above all, there were warnings against complacency regarding the effect on German destiny of American intervention and strong recommendations that caution and restraint be used to keep America out. Exceptional were the reactions of General Friedrich von Boetticher, Germany's military attaché in Washington, whose cheerful political commentary on American weakness, pessimism about Britain and the influence of an isolationist and pro-German "General Staff" were received with pleasure by Hitler. This was what he wished to hear and not the sobering reports of the experts with their tiresome doubts about his intuition.

Early in the war, busy with his initial conquests, Hitler felt no need to take note of America, and as one surveys the concepts and plans of the political leadership of the Reich, the notes of meetings, the diaries, the speeches and comments of the time; when one views the diplomatic and military arrangements and activities which brought Hitler victory after victory in Europe, the influence of the United States seems modest indeed. This may have been reasonable so long as the war was confined to the continent of Europe. But in 1940, Hitler suffered his first reverse: Britain, with whom he had hoped to make an arrangement, refused to surrender. And this resistance brought into play the American influence which Hitler could not merely wave aside. With American support playing an ever-increasing role in the British refusal to capitulate, the vision of an Anglo-Saxon bloc assumed increasing clarity. This was an unanticipated and unwelcome development, and he resisted its implications. Hitler's attention was forced outward and that extraordinary combination of fanatic attachment to goals and opportunistic sense of tactical expedience which had served him so well in Europe began to come unstuck.

## IGNORING THE PROBLEM

He clung on the one hand to his own instincts, so well reflected in Boetticher's image of a weak and divided America whose unlikely intervention could in any event be disregarded in the face of German superiority, while on the other hand the reality of the American commitment, substantiating the reports of the Washington Embassy, imposed upon him the need to take America into account. His solution to the dilemma was altogether typical. He retreated from the whole prospect of naval warfare against the Anglo-Saxons into the comfortable certainties of Operation Barbarossa [the code name for the German invasion of Russia]. Here Roosevelt's appeals could be dismissed with contempt, for even the diplomats were dubious about the possibility of a continental invasion by American military forces. Here the Fuehrer was on home ground, safe in *Festung Europa* [Fortress Europe], untroubled by maritime and other baffling considerations. Still, some policy had to be carried out vis-à-vis the United States pending the final solution of the Russian question. This task he handed over to his navy (whose problems he could not understand) and to the Japanese (whose situation he could not appreciate).

In the Atlantic, the burden of dealing with America fell upon the navy. Against the background of a confused naval tradition and Hitler's relative indifference to naval affairs, which had rendered the navy at once unprepared for the war and subordinate to the other services, the Fuehrer refused to allow his admirals to engage in operations which might provoke the Americans and thereby distract him from his maps of the Ukraine. To his admirals' pleas to challenge the flow of American aid on the high seas, Hitler turned a deaf ear. Requests to apply prize law and open operations within the American security zone were rebuffed. Adopting this unusual posture of restraint, he revealed some inconsistency with his own expressed contempt for American power and he demonstrated even more clearly the dangers implicit

## A RUBBISH HEAP OF A NATION

*In the following excerpt from his book* Hitler's Apocalypse: Jews and the Nazi Legacy, *historian Robert Wistrich depicts Hitler's bad opinion of the United States and its multiethnic culture.*

The American ethnic melting-pot and its vibrant democracy became a symbol to the Nazis of the ruinous effects of race-mixing. America was not a real nation but the centre of a technological rootless 'civilization', of the Hollywood dream factory—a land of millionaires, gangsters, assassins, beauty queens, stupid records and bad taste; its democratic political system was but a hollow façade for Mafia corruption and the rule of a Jew-ridden international plutocracy. This 'Judaized', negrified racial hodge-podge was now ridiculed by Hitler and the Nazis as a rubbish heap composed of the social débris of Europe washed up on its shores. A country which 'had a concept of life inspired by the most vulgar commercialism' and no feeling for such sublime experiences of the human spirit as great music was no place for Hitler, as he confided to Italian dictator Benito Mussolini during one of their wartime meetings. A people which placed profit before blood consisted of the 'lowest kind of rabble'.

Robert Wistrich, *Hitler's Apocalypse: Jews and the Nazi Legacy*, 1985.

in his single-minded fixation with Barbarossa. For the battle of the Atlantic, which he continued to view as a holding operation having little connection with the immediate business at hand, had in fact become a crucially important aspect of the German war effort.

## GERMANY'S SUPPORT OF JAPAN

In the Pacific his instrument for dealing with the Americans was Japan. He had long proclaimed a lack of interest in the Far East, and there was little solid foundation on which to build German-Japanese relations. The 1936 Anti-Comintern Pact between Germany and Japan and the German pressure prior to the war for an alliance were based on the usefulness such arrangements might have for German continental ambitions. As the Anglo-German war continued and American aid increased, he invoked the Far East once again, for even the Washington Embassy had reported on American fear of a two-ocean war. Hitler moved toward the Tripartite Pact between Germany, Japan, and Italy in an attempt to intimidate Roosevelt. Once again, however, the instinct regarding foreign peoples which had served him so well in Europe, but so badly in America, failed him in dealing with an unfamiliar area. For Japan the problem of the United States was of immediate economic and strategic significance. For Hitler it was a nuisance to be held at bay. Japan needed a firm commitment, but also had to move cautiously regarding the Americans. Hitler wanted no Far Eastern commitment for Germany but a threatening stance by the Japanese to subdue the already weak and divided Americans. Hence Japan was encouraged to block American shipping to Russia and expand rapidly to the south in the full knowledge that this would almost certainly provoke an American military response. The Japanese were told of American weakness and encouraged to adopt an unyielding line in their dealings with the United States or preferably to break off the dealings altogether. Finally, the Japanese were given a blank check regarding a Japanese-American war and assured of the fullest German support even in the event of a Japanese attack.

The contradiction between Atlantic caution and Pacific recklessness is notable. There was probably an irreducible element of inconsistency in Hitler's response, doubtless a natural result of the intrusion of an unexpected factor into a mind filled with *idées fixes* [fixed ideas]. But there was also a kind of logic in what Hitler did. British resistance had invoked the American factor, but if the defeat of Russia would, as Hitler believed, have settled the whole question in short order, then it was reasonable for him to measure any response to the secondary American challenge by the effect it would have upon Barbarossa.

The United States could be checked in the Atlantic or in the Pacific. The former, however, had little connection, as far as Hitler could see, with the Eastern campaign. Therefore, it was just not worth provoking the Americans in order to win a subsidiary fight. In the Pacific, however, in areas involving Soviet security interests in the Far East, Hitler could see greater prizes at stake. Here was a chance simultaneously to weaken British interests, to keep the Americans distracted and, especially as Barbarossa slowed, to divert Russian military strength from the German lines. Moreover, in the Pacific someone else's armed forces would have to do the fighting. All of this made the risk of an American entry more worth taking.

## A Crucial Failure

Although these considerations would have been a reasonable basis on which to formulate a comprehensive policy toward the United States, there is no evidence that such an overall strategy was actually worked out. It is doubtful that Hitler would have given that much of his time to the study of a situation which every instinct and selected bit of information told him ought not to have developed at all. It cannot be surprising, then, that there was also no plan for attacking the United States nor for dealing with that country as a military target had Hitler achieved continental fulfillment.

Thus the contradiction between Atlantic hesitation and Pacific provocation as well as the failure adequately to plan for a confrontation with America either before the entry of that country or after history had awarded him his European prize are symptomatic of Hitler's political and military limitations; of his inability to grasp the war as a strategic whole, East and West, on land and sea, in Europe and beyond; of his failure to bridge the gap between immediate military problems and that wider conflict which was looming and which was so much the product of his own policies; of his inadequacy in not rising above his prejudices and fixations when faced with realities which offended him.

It is really doubtful if these problems occurred to him. He remained hunched over his map tables before and after Pearl Harbor, pursuing the final solution to the Russian problem, which would, he knew, either shut out the rash and absurd intrusion of the Americans into German affairs or leave him free to attend to these impossible people as he saw fit. But the Russian question proved insoluble. The shadow of America fell more deeply across *Festung Europa,* because Hitler had first ignored the United States and then, when this became no longer possible, because he did not know how to cope with the implications of American Power.

During the final days in the Berlin bunker, Hitler declared that "The war with America is a tragedy; illogical, devoid of fundamental reality." This is an ironic statement of the matter. For Hitler, the American entry was indeed a tragedy. But American involvement was not illogical, given the circumstances and the use Hitler made of them and it was in fact his own outlook toward that country which had, in the years down through 1941, been "devoid of fundamental reality."

# The Holocaust Cost Hitler Victory in the War

Sebastian Haffner

Sebastian Haffner left his native Germany during the 1930s and worked as a journalist in England for many years. Long after the war, he returned to Germany and wrote *The Meaning of Hitler*, from which the following essay is excerpted. Haffner describes how Hitler ordered the mass exterminations of innocent civilians—not only the Jews but also the Polish and Russian intellectual classes and the nomadic gypsies of Europe. According to Haffner, these mass murders were in no way necessary to Germany's war effort. In fact, he argues, they impeded Germany's military efficiency by diverting manpower and materiel from the battlefield to the concentration camps. Furthermore, Haffner maintains, the brutal liquidations in Russia eliminated the possibility that the Russian people might welcome the Germans as a better alternative than their own oppressive communist government. In the author's opinion, Hitler was so obsessed with eradicating the Jews and other "undesirables" that even after he realized he could not win the war, instead of trying to surrender under agreeable terms for Germany, he drastically increased the operations at the death camps and used the war to conceal these crimes against humanity.

There is no doubt that Adolf Hitler is a figure of world political history; there is equally no doubt that he belongs in the annals of crime. He attempted, albeit unsuccessfully, to establish an empire by wars of conquest. Such an enterprise invariably involves a lot of bloodshed; nevertheless, no one would describe the great conquerors, from Alexander to Napoleon, simply as criminals. Hitler is not a criminal merely because he followed in their footsteps.

## HITLER THE MASS MURDERER

He is a criminal for a totally different reason. Hitler had countless harmless people put to death, for no military or political purpose, but merely for his personal gratification. . . . His victims are counted not in dozens or hundreds but in millions. He was, among other things, quite simply a mass murderer.

Here we are using the term in its precise criminological meaning, not by any means in the rhetorical or polemical sense in which it is sometimes flung in the face of statesmen or generals who send their enemies or their own troops to death. Statesmen (and generals) have at all times and in all countries found themselves in the situation of ordering people to be killed—in war, in civil war, in national crises and at times of revolution. That does not make them criminals. It may be true that nations have always been very sensitive to whether, in committing those deeds, their rulers were only obeying necessity or secretly enjoying themselves. The reputation of *cruel* rulers has always remained tainted even if otherwise they were efficient rulers. This goes, for instance, for Russian leader Joseph Stalin. Hitler, among other things, was also a cruel ruler—which, incidentally, made him something of an exception in German history. Prior to Hitler cruel rulers were far less common in Germany than, for instance, in Russia or France. But this is not the point here. Hitler was cruel not only as a ruler or conqueror. What is special about Hitler is that he had murders committed, and on an unimaginable scale, even when the national interest provided not the slightest reason or even pretext for them. Sometimes, indeed, his mass murders were actually counter to his political and military interests. Thus he might possibly have been able to win the war against Russia politically—a war which, as we now know, could never have been won militarily—if he had appeared as a liberator [of the Russians from communism] instead of an exterminator. But his lust for murder was even stronger than his by no means slight ability for political calculation.

## HARMFUL TO GERMANY'S WAR EFFORT

Hitler's mass murders were committed during the war but they were not acts of war. On the contrary, it may be said that he used the war as a pretext for committing mass murders which had nothing to do with the war, but for which he had always felt a personal need. 'If the best men were killed at the front,' he had written in *Mein Kampf,* 'then at home one could at least exterminate the vermin.' The extermination of those human beings who were vermin to Hitler was related to the war only in the sense that the war diverted attention from it. Otherwise it was, to Hitler, an end in itself and in no way a means to victory or the averting of defeat.

On the contrary, it impeded the conduct of the war because thousands of SS men, who were fit for active service but who were engaged on this operation, were lacking at the front—all in all the equivalent of several divisions—, and because the daily mass transports to the extermination camps, right across Europe, were depriving the fighting forces of an appreciable amount of rolling stock which was in short supply and which was urgently needed for supplies. And once victory could no longer be won, the murder operations rendered impossible any compromise peace because as the facts became increasingly known they convinced the statesmen, first in the West and then also in Russia, that the war could be meaningfully concluded not by any diplomatic transaction *with* Hitler but only by court action *against* him. The war aim of 'punishment of those responsible for the crimes', proclaimed by the Western Allies in January 1942 and eventually also by the Soviet Union in November 1943, entailed the further war aim of unconditional surrender. . . .

## HITLER'S CRIMES AGAINST HUMANITY

It is with these crimes of Hitler that we now have to concern ourselves. I intend to spare the reader the description of the horrible details. They are amply described in other books. We shall confine ourselves here to setting out the facts in chronological sequence.

1. Hitler's written order for the mass killing of invalids in Germany bears the date of 1 September 1939, the day of the outbreak of war. On the strength of this order roughly 100,000 Germans—'useless eaters'—were officially put to death over the next two years. In detail these were 70,000 to 80,000 patients in medical and nursing institutions, 10,000 to 20,000 segregated invalids and disabled people in concentration camps, all the Jewish patients in psychiatric hospitals, and roughly 3,000 children between the ages of three and thirteen, mainly in special schools or requiring special care. The operation was suspended in August 1941, partly

because it had been causing growing disquiet among the population and had given rise to public protests from the Churches, and partly—perhaps chiefly—because the organization set up for the implementation of the liquidation of the sick (code name T4) was needed by Hitler for the extermination of the Jews which was then being launched on a major scale. Later there was no opportunity for resuming the extermination of the sick.

## LIQUIDATING THE GIPSIES

2. The extermination of the gipsies likewise began in Germany in September 1939. They were being rounded up everywhere and first moved to concentration camps and then, in two operations, in 1941 and 1943, transferred to extermination camps. From 1941 onwards the gipsies in the occupied countries of Eastern Europe were being as systematically liquidated as the Jews living there. This mass murder—perhaps because it had never been heralded or accompanied by propaganda but had taken place quietly—has scarcely been researched in detail even now. It was not talked about while it was taking place, and to this day we do not know much more about it than that it did take place. Records are scarce. Estimates of the total numbers murdered go as high as 500,000. At any rate of the 25,000 gipsies living in Germany in 1939 only about 5,000 were alive in 1945.

## MASS MURDER IN POLAND

3. About one month later, in October 1939, following the termination of military operations in Poland, Hitler's third series of mass murders began. This time the victims were the Polish intelligentsia and leading strata of society. This operation continued throughout five long years. Here we have no written order by Hitler—the written order for the extermination of the sick was the last of its kind—but only verbal instructions which, however, are equally well attested and were equally strictly implemented. SS General Reinhard Heydrich, for instance, in a report dated 2 July 1940 on complaints from the Wehrmacht (the armed forces) about the German reign of terror in Poland, refers to an 'extraordinarily radical special order of the Führer' (e.g. an order to liquidate numerous Polish leading classes, running into thousands of people), and the Governor-General of occupied Poland, Hans Frank, quotes a verbal reminder by Hitler

dated 30 May 1940: 'Whatever leading stratum we have now identified in Poland must be liquidated; whatever moves up into its place must be secured by us and again removed after an appropriate space of time.' It is an established fact that, upon Hitler's instructions, throughout the next five years not only Jews but also non-Jewish Poles were stripped of their rights and put at the mercy of totally arbitrary rule, and that in particular the members of the educated classes—priests, teachers, professors, journalists, entrepreneurs—fell victim to a systematic campaign of eradication. . . .

The precise number of educated Poles who fell victim to this systematic mass murder is more difficult to establish than that of the murdered Jews. Altogether, according to official Polish data, Poland, over the six years of the war, lost approximately six million people, of whom roughly three million were murdered Jews. No more than 300,000 Poles were killed in action. If one adds 700,000 to account for refugees and natural wastage, that leaves two million of whom certainly more than half are accounted for by the systematic extermination measures against the leading classes. The remainder can probably be ascribed to reprisals in the war against the partisans, to the mass population transfers which were executed with extreme ruthlessness, and to the general intimidation and terrorization by the occupation authorities.

## ATROCITIES IN RUSSIA

4. German policy with regard to the Russian population in the vast Russian territories occupied throughout two or three years was entirely in line with the Polish policy just described: extermination of leading strata, deprivation of rights and enslavement of the remaining mass of the population. . . . In the case of Russia, however, there were two differences which further exacerbated this policy.

Firstly, the Russian upper classes were—in reality or by assumption—communist, whereas those of Poland had predominantly been conservative and Catholic, and this meant the dropping of whatever inhibitions were left about their systematic extermination. Secondly, in contrast to their attitude to Poland the Wehrmacht was a willing participant in the crimes committed in Russia. . . .

According to a survey of the Wehrmacht General Office in the High Command of the Armed Forces of 1 May 1944, 5.16 million Russians had been taken prisoner up to that date, most of them in the first campaign of 1941. Of these 1,871,000 were still alive at that date; 473,000 were listed as 'executed', and 67,000 as escaped. The rest—nearly three million—had died in the POW cages, mostly starved to death. . . .

The mass murder of Russian civilians belonging to the leading strata was not the task of the Wehrmacht but that of four Special Operations Units which had been conducting the murder business behind the lines at high pressure from the first day onwards. By April 1942—that is, over the first ten months of a four-year war—Special Operations Unit A (North) reported 250,000 'executed'; Special Operations Unit B (Centre) 70,000; Special Operations Unit C (South) 150,000; and Special Operations Unit D (extreme Southern Front) 90,000. As later figures have not reached us and as the reports do not differentiate between Jews and 'Bolsheviks', it is difficult to estimate the precise total of murdered non-Jewish Russian civilians. But it is certainly not likely to be lower than that in Poland—if anything, higher. We have already observed that by this mass murder Hitler, far from improving his chances of victory, on the contrary wrecked them.

## THE JEWISH HOLOCAUST

5. Hitler's most extensive mass murder, as is well known, was committed against the Jews. At first, after mid-1941, this was against the Jews of Poland and Russia, and then, after the beginning of 1942, also against the Jews of Germany and the whole of occupied Europe which was, for this purpose, 'combed through from West to East'. The wished-for aim announced by Hitler in advance on 30 January 1939 was 'the annihilation of the Jewish race in Europe'. This final aim was not achieved, in spite of extreme efforts. Even so, the total of Jews murdered at Hitler's command amounts, according to the lowest calculations, to more than four million and according to the highest to nearly six million. Until 1942 the murders were carried out by mass shooting before mass graves which the victims had previously been forced to dig; subsequently in the six extermination camps of Treblinka, Sobibor, Maidanek (Lublin), Belzec, Chelmno (Kulmhof) and Auschwitz, by gassing in specially constructed gas chambers to which huge crematoria were attached.

An English historian, David Irving, has disputed Hitler's responsibility for the murder of the Jews, which, Irving claims, was performed by SS Commander Heinrich Himmler on his own initiative behind Hitler's back. Irving's thesis is untenable not only because it lacks all internal probability—under the conditions of the Third Reich it was totally impossible for an operation on that scale to be carried out without the knowledge, let alone against the wishes, of Hitler, not to mention the fact that Hitler himself had proclaimed in advance the 'annihilation of the Jewish race' in the event of war—but also because clear testimony, both of Hitler and of Himmler, proves that Hitler had given the orders and Himmler had executed them. Hitler publicly boasted of the implementation of his forecast on no fewer than five occasions in the course of 1942 (the first year of the 'Final Solution'): on 1 January, on 30 January, on 24 February, on 30 September and on 8 November. We shall quote the last statement verbatim:

> You may still remember the meeting of the Reichstag [parliament] when I declared: In case Jewry imagines that it can trigger off an international world war for the extermination of the European races, then the outcome will be not the extermination of the European races but the extermination of Jewry in Europe. I have always been laughed at as a prophet. Of those who then laughed a countless number are no longer laughing today, and those who are still laughing will perhaps no longer be doing so in a little while.

### HITLER'S NOTE TO HIMMLER

. . . Irving's only evidence in support of his thesis is a note made by Himmler on 30 November 1941, after a headquarter's conversation with Hitler: 'Jewish transport from Berlin, no liquidation.' In this one instance Hitler evidently ordered an exception to be made, which in itself proves that 'liquidation' was the rule and, moreover, that Hitler concerned himself even with the details of this murder operation. It is also easy to see why the exception was made; the Jewish transport from Berlin had been premature; it was not yet the turn of the German Jews. In November 1941 the 'liquidation' of the Polish and Russian Jews was still in full swing whereas the 'Final Solution' for the whole of Europe was not organized until the Wannsee Conference of 20 January 1942, and there had to be order in everything. Besides, the gas chambers and cremating furnaces were not yet ready. They only went into operation, one at a time, in 1942. . . .

The date [of the note concerning the Jewish transport from Berlin] is interesting. It is five days before the Russian counter-offensive at Moscow, which convinced Hitler that the war could no longer be won; ten days before his declaration of war on America, with which he sealed his defeat; and fifty days before the Wannsee Conference at which the 'Final Solution of the Jewish problem' was organized, that is, the murder of the Jews in Germany, as well as the rest of Europe, in death factories. Until then the systematic murder of the Jews had been confined to Poland and Russia, and its cumbersome method had been mass shooting.

There is a clear connection between the three dates. So long as Hitler was still hoping to achieve in Russia a similarly rapid victory as a year before in France, he was also hoping that Britain would come to terms since in Russia she would have lost her last 'continental sword'. He had often said so. But in that case he must not appear as a mass murderer in countries where anything that happened became instantly known in Britain. What he was doing in Poland and in Russia could, so he had reason to hope, be kept secret from the outside world at least while the war was on, but mass murder in France, Holland, Belgium, Luxembourg, Denmark, Norway, and even Germany itself, would become immediately known in Britain and would make Hitler totally unacceptable there—which is what actually happened. The proclamation of 'punishment for these crimes' as a new Western war aim dates from January 1942.

In other words, Hitler would only be able to fulfil his long-cherished wish to exterminate the Jews from the whole of Europe if he abandoned all hope of a negotiated peace with Britain (and the associated hope of preventing America from joining the war). And that he only did after 5 December 1941, the day when the Russian offensive at Moscow rudely awakened him from his dreams of victory in Russia. This must have come as an extraordinary shock to him; only two months previously he had publicly announced 'that this opponent is already on the ground and will never rise again'. And under the impact of that shock he now changed course, 'icily cold' and 'quick as lightning'. If he could no longer be victorious in Russia then, so Hitler argued, there was also no chance left of peace with Britain. He might therefore also declare war on America straight away, a step which, after U.S. President Franklin Roosevelt's long unanswered provocations, gave him patent satisfaction. And he could also indulge in the even greater satisfaction of giving orders now for the

'Final Solution of the Jewish problem' for the whole of Europe, since he no longer needed to consider the effect that this crime would have in Britain or America. At the same time he also made Germany's defeat inevitable and moreover ensured that defeat would be followed by judgement. . . .

## HITLER'S CHOICE

In short, in December 1941, within a few days, Hitler made his final choice between the two incompatible aims which he had pursued from the outset—German domination of the world and the extermination of the Jews. He abandoned the former as unattainable and entirely concentrated on the latter. (On 30 November it had still been a few days too early for that.) Moreover, he now even accepted Germany's total defeat with all the possible consequences as the price of being able to carry out at last the extermination of the Jews throughout Europe, a plan which had long made his mouth water. . . .

What Hitler continued to concern himself with, and more intensively than ever, was the military conduct of the war. This he still needed in order to gain the time in which to carry out his intended mass murder and to hold the territory in which he found his victims. His strategy in the years after 1942 was exclusively aimed at gaining time and holding territory. Initiatives for spectacular isolated military successes, such as might have given a man other than Hitler a chance of a negotiated peace, Hitler no longer developed after the beginning of 1943. Whenever individual generals took such initiatives . . . he no longer supported them. If anything, he obstructed them. They no longer interested him.

All the evidence is that since the turn of the year 1941/42 he had inwardly come to terms with eventual defeat. Indeed his still famous statement, rather revealing in its ambiguity, 'As a matter of principle I never stop until five minutes past twelve', dates from November 1942. The fact that, throughout these years, while the ring around Germany was closing ever more tightly, he continued in his table talk at headquarters to reveal an often unimpaired self-satisfaction and at times even robust merriment, can only be explained by his knowledge that his now sole objective was moving closer towards realization every day, just as the Allied armies were drawing closer to a gutted and bombed Germany. For three years, day after day, Jewish families throughout Europe were taken from their homes or hiding places, transported to the East and driven naked into the death factories, where the chimneys of the cremating furnaces smoked day and night. During those three years Hitler no longer enjoyed successes, as during the preceding eleven years. However, he found it easy to do without them since, more than ever before, he was now able to indulge the delights of the killer who has shed his last restraints, has his victims in his grip and deals with them as he wishes.

To Hitler, during the last three and a half years of war, the war had become a kind of race which he was still hoping to win. Who would reach his goal sooner, Hitler with his extermination of the Jews or the Allies with their military overthrow of Germany? It took the Allies three and a half years to reach their goal. And in the meantime Hitler, too, had certainly come terrifyingly close to his.

# Hitler Gradually Developed the Idea of the Final Solution

William Carr

The late William Carr was a professor at the University of Sheffield in England and the author of *Hitler: A Study in Personality and Politics,* from which the following reading is excerpted. In Carr's view, while Adolf Hitler was undoubtedly an anti-Semite early in his political career, he did not originally intend to kill all the Jews of Europe in the death camps. Carr traces the gradual acceleration of anti-Jewish legislation and violence promulgated by the Nazi Party, noting that Hitler frequently reined in the more radical party members. Although Hitler was eager to rid Germany of the Jews, he initially thought in terms of relocating the Jewish population to the Urals in Russia or to the African island of Madagascar, Carr writes. He asserts that Hitler only abandoned these plans as developments during World War II prevented them from being carried out.

It is sometimes supposed even today that Nazi policy towards the Jews had from beginning to end only one objective in view, and that it moved with relentless logic from the first anti-Jewish demonstrations in April 1933 to the 'Final Solution' in the death camps of Poland. The very enormity of the holocaust encouraged men to search for a 'grand design' or 'master plan' which could be attributed to Adolf Hitler's personal predilections. Closer examination of the record suggests a rather different pattern, more in keeping with what we know of the highly personalized style of government and the shifting power structure of the Third Reich. On balance it seems much more likely that the pressure of external events, internal power configurations and the influence of powerful

Excerpted from *Hitler: A Study in Personality and Politics,* by William Carr. Copyright © William Carr 1979. Reprinted with the permission of St. Martin's Press, Inc.

individuals were just as important as Hitler's personal inclinations and the inherent radicalism of the Nazi Party in determining the policy adopted by the regime.

## POPULAR MEASURES

Legislation to restrict the freedom of what the Nazis were pleased to call 'alien elements' in German society aroused little disquiet in middle-class circles. The fact is that in no significant particular did the anti-semitic programme of the Nazi Party break new ground. Other right-wing groups were equally anxious to deny citizenship to Jews, expel those Jews who had entered Germany since 1914, and remove all Jews from public office and from the newspaper world. Hitler could, therefore, rely on general support from the broad middle class for the first anti-semitic measures in April and June 1933, which excluded Jews from the civil service and legal profession, restricted their entry into schools and universities, and empowered the government to revoke German citizenship and confiscate the property of Jewish émigrés.

Such difficulties as Hitler faced were caused by party activists dissatisfied with these 'modest' beginnings. Many rank-and-file members were filled with a lively hatred of things semitic and itched to use physical violence against individual Jews and their property. For tactical reasons this intestinal anti-semitism had been held in check between 1930 and 1933. But in the hectic atmosphere of the 'March Days' exuberant activists, with the full backing of the party press, took to the streets, demonstrated noisily for a 'Jew-free' economy, assaulted Jews and invaded court houses demanding the immediate removal of all Jewish lawyers— with whom many of these Brownshirted hooligans had crossed swords in the past. The evidence is too slender to decide whether street pressure was unwelcome to a new chancellor anxious to impress cabinet colleagues and foreign powers with his statesmanlike moderation, or whether he secretly rejoiced and encouraged excesses in the hope that conservatives in the cabinet might be forced to go further. Of his own radical instincts there is little doubt. On the eve of power, while carefully avoiding public attacks on Jewry, he reiterated in private the party's commitment to racial discrimination adding darkly that, if the Jews persisted in propagating democratic ideas, pogroms would 'hit them harder than those described in their Biblical past'. . . .

## THE NUREMBERG LAWS

The next important extension of the anti-semitic legislation, the notorious Nuremberg Laws of 1935, was introduced in somewhat dramatic circumstances. In the middle of the party rally Hitler, without consulting cabinet colleagues or permanent officials, suddenly summoned Bernhard Lösener, the civil servant responsible for Jewish affairs in the ministry of the interior, and several of his colleagues to Nuremberg and ordered them to draft on the spot new laws regulating sexual relations between Jews and Gentiles—an aspect of anti-semitism which pornographic anti-semitic publications such as *Der Stürmer* dwelt upon at great length. At a specially convened Reichstag [parliament] on 15 September three new laws were promulgated: the first forbade Jews to fly the national flag; the second defined German citizenship; and the third—the so-called law for the protection of German blood and honour—prohibited marriage and extramarital relations between Jews and Gentiles.

One should be careful not to exaggerate the significance of Hitler's initiative. Legislation of this kind had long been anticipated in the ministry of the interior. And from the end of 1934 a wave of popular anti-semitism gave a proleptic hint to the discerning of what was to come. The agitation, actively encouraged by Minister of Propaganda Joseph Goebbels, the most influential anti-semite in Hitler's immediate entourage, mounted in intensity in the summer of 1935. Possibly Hitler was not unmindful of the damage anti-semitic excesses could do to Germany's international standing, now greatly improved after the Anglo-German Naval Convention. On 8 August Hitler forbade undisciplined acts by party members, a theme taken up by Minister of the Interior Wilhelm Frick who a few days later threatened offenders with severe penalties. However, once Hitler had reasserted his authority over the party and the anti-semitic agitation died away in the high summer, he was prepared once again to gratify the wishes of the activists. . . .

The plight of the Jews would have worsened more rapidly than it did between 1935 and 1937 had it not been for two factors, neither of Hitler's making. In the first place ministry officials, sticklers for the law like civil servants the world over, strenuously opposed illegal interpretations placed on these laws by zealous party members. Hitler did nothing to discourage these encroachments, and seems to have welcomed them.

What is interesting is that Hitler did not support the party members against the officials. Furthermore, on at least three occasions in 1937, because of technical objections raised in the ministries of finance and the interior, Hitler shelved legislation which he had personally initiated. Secondly, Hitler and his associates still felt the need to respect world opinion. That was no doubt the reason why, when a high Nazi official was assassinated in Switzerland by a Jew in February 1936, Hitler, on the eve of the Rhineland re-occupation, suppressed his natural instinct to deliver a blistering anti-semitic funeral oration. He seems also to have been concerned about the possibility of anti-semitic outbursts endangering the prestigious Olympic Games to be held in Germany in the summer and winter of 1936. It was on his personal orders that anti-Jewish slogans were removed and the display of *Der Stürmer* banned for the duration of the Games. . . .

## VIOLENT OUTBURSTS AND NEW RESTRICTIONS

The radical changes that were on the way were revealed starkly during Reichskristallnacht [the Night of Broken Glass] on 9–10 November 1938. Ninety Jews were murdered, synagogues all over Germany went up in flames, and 7,000 Jewish shops were destroyed in an unprecedented outburst of frightful savagery organized by party activists. . . .

As usual Hitler avoided direct involvement in the savagery, leaving Goebbels to organize 'spontaneous' demonstrations in villages and towns throughout the length and breadth of Germany. It is significant that Hitler did not inform Reichstag President Hermann Goering, Heinrich Himmler or Reinhard Heydrich his deputy—all deeply interested in the fate of German Jewry—of the pogrom because he obviously realized that they would oppose it. Goering, a long standing rival of Goebbels and resentful of the latter's ambition, protested to Hitler about the damage done to the economy. Himmler and Heydrich were equally critical of its adverse effect on emigration plans. But all attempts to engineer Goebbels's dismissal misfired. Hitler ostentatiously demonstrated complete solidarity with the propaganda minister, and the protests died away. In any case the whole Nazi hierarchy was very soon absorbed in the congenial task of hedging Jews around with new restrictions. . . .
A spate of discriminatory and often spiteful legislation deprived them of the means of livelihood: a huge fine of 1,000

million marks was imposed on them; all Jewish firms and real estate holdings were compulsorily sold; Jews were forced to surrender all shares and gold and silver possessions; they were totally excluded from schools and universities and even from cinemas, theatres and concert halls, sports stadia and swimming pools; and by 1939 able-bodied and unemployed Jews were forced into labour battalions engaged on public works. The evidence suggests that Hitler took a lively personal interest in these measures. . . .

As the war clouds gathered, there were ugly signs that the Nazi leadership was prepared to make the Jews pay a heavy price should hostilities break out. Nevertheless, it is probably an oversimplification of a complex situation to construe Hitler's bloodthirsty and ferocious comments to foreign statesmen as an unequivocal commitment to the physical annihilation of the Jews at the earliest possible moment. Even the celebrated remark in the Reichstag on 30 January 1939 that, if 'international Jewish finance' plunged the world into war, the result would not be 'the bolshevization of the earth and the victory of Jewry' but 'the annihilation of the Jewish race in Europe', might be interpreted either as a blunt warning to Germany's enemies that the Jews would not be spared the horrors of war or perhaps as a clumsy attempt to put the blame for war on the Jews. One must resist the temptation to read back into Hitler's remarks sinister undertones of a policy not decided on until 1941. Just as one must pay due regard to 'alternative' foreign policies which to some extent modified Hitler's own concepts, so, too, in studying the holocaust one must allow for the possibility that there were other 'final solutions' before the gas chambers.

## LOOKING FOR A SOLUTION

The weight of the evidence suggests that Hitler had no very clear idea of what should be done with the Jews apart from turning them into pariahs. Therefore, he was perfectly prepared to fall in with whatever 'solution' of the 'Jewish problem' was currently in vogue in the corridors of power. Emigration is a case in point. Hitler looked with favour on this solution because it was supported by Himmler, a rising star in the Nazi firmament. By combining high office in the party with control of the German police, Himmler had turned the SS into an organization of immense power by the late 1930s. One of the units under his command, the Sicherheitsdienst, or SS Security Service, happened to have been sponsoring the emigration of Jews to Palestine since 1935. In February 1938 Hitler gave his formal approval to this policy despite foreign office objections to the creation of a Zionist state in the Middle East. That Hitler, who may in the first place have been following the line of least resistance, became convinced of the viability of this 'solution' is suggested by his approval of private negotiations . . . which Minister of Economics Hjaldemar Schacht was allowed to conduct in 1938–9 with George Rublee, the chairman of the International Committee for Political Refugees; this was an (unsuccessful) attempt to finance the emigration of 150,000 German Jews through Jewish payments for German exports. And in January 1939, when Goering called for the acceleration of emigration 'by every possible means', he clearly had Hitler's approval. The fact that a total of 247,000 of Germany's 503,000 Jews had left Grossdeutschland [Greater Germany] by September 1939—78,000 in that year alone—is proof that the Nazis pursued this policy with energy and conviction. Far from holding on to the Jews as an insurance policy to keep foreign powers off their backs, the Nazis did their best to be rid of the 'plague bacilli'.

The brutalization of life which war brings in its wake could not fail to affect the position of the Jews, now virtually outcasts in German society. Proof beyond all doubt that Hitler was a man of instinctive violence capable of the most frightful deeds came at the beginning of the Polish campaign: he ordered four special commandos into Poland in the wake of the German armies with orders to execute thousands of prominent citizens, in a cold-blooded attempt to destroy the fabric of the Polish ruling class. No specific order to execute Jews was given but the Einsatzgruppen, or special commandos, took it upon themselves to shoot any Jews they could find. When the military authorities protested at the disastrous effect these horrors were having on army morale, and Himmler restrained the murder gangs, Hitler at once intervened and relieved the military of all responsibility for the civilian population, making it abundantly clear that he would tolerate no criticism of Himmler's work. By the end of the year the special commandos had recommenced their indiscriminate shootings.

Even so, the systematic extermination of the Jewish race was probably not finalized in Hitler's mind at this stage. As emigration was impracticable while the British fleet ruled the seas, Hitler seems to have toyed with some other 'territorial' solution to the problem. While the Einsatzgruppen were still at work in September 1939, he informed Himmler, Heydrich, Danzig district head Albert Forster and later Nazi racial theorist Alfred Rosenberg that he wanted all Polish Jews—some three million in all—to be concentrated in ghettos in specified towns (to facilitate overall control of them), as a prelude to the creation of a huge Jewish reserve between the rivers Vistula and Bug, that is on the eastern frontier of the new Reich. On 7 October Himmler was given full powers as Reichs commissioner for the strengthening of Germanism (in other words, for settling Germans in the conquered territories) to carry out this task—a sure sign of Hitler's complete confidence in the Reichsführer SS. Between December 1939 and February 1940 large numbers of Jews were transported to the area south of Lublin which the Reichssicherheitshauptamt, the headquarters of the SS security service, had earmarked as the reserve.

This 'final solution' lasted barely six months. Quite why Hitler lost faith in it is a mystery. It is hardly conceivable that he turned against it because overcrowding in the reserve would make it impossible for the Jews to maintain tolerable living standards. Probably Goering informed him of Polish Governor Hans Frank's representations in February 1940 that the transportation of Jews should be halted because of the intolerable strain being placed on limited food supplies in German-occupied Poland. It is safe to assume that when Goering finally stopped all transportation on 24 March 1940 it was with Hitler's approval.

Three months later, during the closing stages of the French campaign, Hitler toyed momentarily with a second territorial solution—the so-called Madagascar plan. The proposal, worked out in a foreign office memorandum, was to ship all western Jews to Madagascar, leaving the eastern Jews in Poland as a pledge of continuing American neutrality. Himmler was immediately enthusiastic, a factor which probably weighed heavily with Hitler, and with the Führer's approval the Reichssicherheitshauptamt drafted a scheme for transporting three-and-a-half million Jews to the island after the war. During the summer Hitler mentioned the plan to several prominent figures including Italian dictator Benito Mussolini, Admiral Erich Raeder and Otto Abetz, German ambassador in Paris. As late as June 1941 he told a Croatian collaborator that he intended to send all the Jews to Madagascar or Siberia. The fact that he was still talking of the Madagascar plan to close friends in the summer of 1942, when extermination was already under way, certainly weakens the argument but does not necessarily mean that he was not in earnest in 1940. Had Britain surrendered that summer, the plan could have been implemented.

## THE BEGINNINGS OF THE HOLOCAUST

It is just possible that a third 'solution' may have crossed Hitler's mind briefly in the summer of 1941 when Russian collapse seemed imminent—the creation of a Jewish reserve in eastern Russia. True, the special commandos employed in Russia had express orders from Hitler to shoot political commissars . . . and Jews. But can one conclude from this that Hitler had finally decided to annihilate the whole of European Jewry? After all, the mass executions in the summer of 1941 were essentially a more horrific version of what had been done in Poland in the autumn of 1939, the difference being that this time 'the Jewish-Bolshevik ruling class' was the main target, even if the men in the Einsatzgruppen ignored this subtle distinction and shot Jews wherever they found them regardless of their status in Soviet society. And in August, speaking to Goebbels, one of the very few men with whom he was brutally frank on the subject of the Jews, Hitler remarked that when transport was again available the Berlin Jews must be shipped to the east where they would have to live in a much harder climate. And in mid-September when Hitler informed Himmler of his decision to free Germany and the Protectorate of all Jews, the Reichsführer SS assumed that this would be a preparatory step to a territorial solution in the east. It could be, as [U.D. Adam] maintains, that Hitler's attitude was not all that different from that of Rosenberg, who declared in November 1941 that the Jewish question would not be solved until the entire Jewish population was biologically extirpated and that to expedite this the Jews must be forced across the Urals. It is just possible that Hitler did not decide upon the direct physical extermination of European Jewry until late October–early November 1941 when his current policy was set on collision course. In the face of stiffening Russian resistance all hope of settling the Jews east of the Urals vanished for the foreseeable future. Yet precisely at this point, when doubts were beginning to assail him, Hitler ordered an acceleration of the deportation, greatly slowed down since the first half of 1941 when preparations for the attack on Russia had prior claim on available transport. In October the first mass deportations from German cities to Lodz commenced. Had the entire Jewish population of Europe—three million Polish Jews and two million from other lands—been crowded into the ghettos of Poland an intolerable situation would have arisen. It did not, because Hitler opted instead for extermination.

The decision was not so much a rational and cold-blooded response to an unforeseen situation forced on an unwilling head of state—though an element of this may perhaps have been present—as a visceral reaction by a fanatical racist determined to be rid of the Jews, *so oder so* [one way or another]. What is interesting from the point of view of Hitler's personality is that he had not just allowed an emergency situation to arise through negligence or preoccupation with more pressing military matters. On the contrary, he had deliberately deepened the crisis by accelerating the deportations. One is reminded of other occasions . . . when he purposely sought confrontation as if to overcome his own doubts and hesitations about the course of action he was about to embark upon.

### THE WAR WITH RUSSIA AND THE HOLOCAUST

Now that Germany was at war with the 'Jewish-Bolshevik' state, . . . it was psychologically much easier to take the decision to murder millions of Jews. Physical extermination of the enemy must have appeared to Hitler as nothing more than a logical extension of the life-and-death struggle against the same enemy without the walls. But what made it objectively possible to turn a nightmare into sober fact—and this was a factor of the utmost importance—was the existence of a highly organized police apparatus controlled by another fanatical racist and a man thoroughly loyal to the Führer. Himmler's Einsatzgruppen had already proved their mettle and were, by sheer coincidence, beginning in the autumn of 1941 to experiment with gas, a silent and swift method of execution making it technically feasible to dispose of millions rather than thousands of victims. In short, the machinery of destruction and the accomplices to operate it already existed, thus enabling Hitler to realize his ambition to 'expel' the Jews from Europe despite a worsening external situation.

Once committed to this barbarous course, Hitler showed no sign of relenting. In private conversation he avoided the subject out of a need to preserve the utmost secrecy. As mentioned above, he pretended on occasions that emigration was the solution he still favoured. Of course, there is little doubt that Hitler was, as Goebbels remarked, 'the undismayed champion of the radical solution both in work and deed'. As late as 1943 he emphasized to Himmler how necessary it was to continue deportations regardless of the unrest it might cause. As the balance of military advantage turned decisively against Germany, he remained as obstinately determined as ever to win at least one battle—the fight against Jewry. And at the very end of his life he claimed with pride that the extirpation of Jewry was his legacy to the world.

## An Act of Sheer Madness

The holocaust is the most macabre monument in the whole of modern history to the power of a myth over the minds of men. The extermination of the Jews made neither economic nor strategic sense. It seems an act of sheer madness to have allocated transport desperately needed on the eastern front to this wholly negative operation. Nor did it make any kind of sense to deprive Germany of a labour force which could have benefited the war effort. However, what to a rational mind is proof of the ultimate irrationality of the Third Reich must be seen—if historians are to make sense of the holocaust and of Hitler's leading role in it—as a logical though not necessarily inevitable outcome of the Nazi belief in the cosmic struggle between the Aryan race and world Jewry. There is an eerie parallel between the attitude of the ruling élite in Nazi Germany to their frightful task and the Aztec priests of old. As is well known, the latter offered up blood sacrifices to appease their gods and prevent darkness and disaster engulfing the Aztec people. It is, to say the least, an arresting thought that members of the special commandos often calmed their troubled consciences with the reassuring thought that the 'execution' of the Jewish 'criminals' would usher in an era of peace for mankind.

Only in 1944, in a broadcast to the German people on 30 January, the anniversary of his coming to power, did Hitler at last raise a corner of the veil of secrecy surrounding the macabre operation and attempt to justify it as a 'historical necessity'. Anti-semitism was most definitely for export in the universal struggle against Jewry. Scornfully he dismissed the opinion that any state could ever come to terms with their Jews any more than the human body could assimilate 'plague bacilli' in the long run. In a chilling phrase he spoke of his hope that other nations might become acquainted with 'the elements of a scientific understanding and objective solution of the [Jewish] question'. And he expressed the hope that the war would 'open the eyes of the peoples in a few years to the Jewish question and the National Socialist answer and the measures for its solution will seem as worthy of emulation as they are a matter of common sense. The greatness of this world historical struggle will train the eyes and minds of the nations for thinking and acting in mighty historical dimensions.'

# The Final Solution Was Always Hitler's Ultimate Goal

Lucy S. Dawidowicz

The late Lucy S. Dawidowicz was a history professor at Yeshiva University in New York City and the author of several books, including *The War Against the Jews, 1933–1945*, from which the following selection is taken. Dawidowicz disagrees with those historians who believe that Hitler did not originally intend to exterminate Europe's Jewish population. She argues that the Holocaust was Hitler's highest priority at least by the early 1920s and probably as far back as November 1918, when he swore to avenge the German defeat in World War I by eliminating the Jewish "traitors" that he held responsible. Hitler realized that he could not openly admit this early in his political career, Dawidowicz contends, so he used euphemisms, double-meanings, and code words that would hide his intentions from all but the Nazi inner circle. Hitler did clearly express his plan for the Final Solution in *Mein Kampf*, Dawidowicz points out, but few people took his book seriously. She concedes that during the 1930s and 1940s, Hitler often seemed to hesitate or waffle about his policy toward the Jews, but she makes the case that he did so only to conceal his unswerving determination to see the Holocaust through to its grisly end.

The Final Solution had its origins in Adolf Hitler's mind. In *Mein Kampf* he tells us that he decided on his war against the Jews in November 1918, when, at the military hospital in Pasewalk, he learned, in rapid succession, of the naval mutiny at Kiel, the revolution that forced the abdication of the Emperor, and finally the armistice. "Everything went

Excerpted from *The War Against the Jews, 1933–1945*, by Lucy S. Dawidowicz. Copyright ©1975 by Lucy S. Dawidowicz. Reprinted by permission of Henry Holt and Company.

black before my eyes," he wrote. In the ensuing "terrible days and even worse nights," while he pondered the meaning of these cataclysmic events, "my own fate became known to me." It was then that he made his decision:

> There is no making pacts with Jews; there can be only the hard: either—or.
>
> I, for my part, decided to go into politics.

Did Hitler really decide then, in November 1918, on the destruction of the Jews as his political goal? Or did the idea remain buried in his mind until it took shape in *Mein Kampf*, which he wrote in 1924? *Mein Kampf* was the basic treatise of Hitler's ideas, where he brought together the three essential components that formed the embryonic concept of the Final Solution. Each component originated in a politically commonplace notion that Hitler transformed into an inordinately radical one. First, he turned political anti-Semitism into a racial doctrine whose purpose was the destruction of the Jews. Second, having defined Bolshevism [Russian communism] as a Jewish conspiracy for world rule, he transformed anti-Bolshevism into a holy crusade to liberate Russia from its allegedly Jewish masters. Third, using race as a rationale, he transformed the imperialist drive for autarky and world power into the concept of Lebensraum [living space]. These three notions were consolidated into a unified concept that became the theoretical, ideational foundation of the Final Solution. In *Mein Kampf* that concept appeared in its matured form and remained a central tenet in Hitler's ideology from which he never deviated. It was already then a fixed idea, in both the everyday and psychiatric meaning of the term, awaiting only the political opportunities for its implementation.

## USING INDIRECT LANGUAGE

If *Mein Kampf* is the *terminus ad quem* [final destination] for the conception of the Final Solution, does its beginning indeed go back to November 1918, as Hitler himself claimed? It is a hazardous task to construct a chronology of the evolution of this idea in Hitler's mind. The historical evidence is sparse and no doubt would be inadmissible as courtroom evidence. The very idea of the destruction of the Jews as a political goal demanded, when Hitler first began to advocate it, camouflage and concealment. Its later consummation demanded, within limits, secrecy. Consequently there is a paucity of documents, and even those we have handicap the search for definitive evidence because of the problem of esoteric language. . . .

In all periods of history, when government or society has put limits on public discussion, those who wish to circumvent censorship resort to the use of esoteric language. Exoterically understood, the text is unexceptionable, but to the insiders who know how to interpret the words, the message is revolutionary and dangerous to the status quo. . . .

According to the earliest reports of Hitler's speeches, the code words he used for Jews outnumbered the plain references: usury (usurers), profiteering (profiteerers), exploiters, big capitalism (big capitalists), international big and/or loan capital, international money power, Communists, Social Democrats, November criminals, revolution criminals, aliens, foreigners. References to the press unmistakably were meant and interpreted as "Jewish" press. In one circumlocution, Hitler spoke of the fight "against the races [*sic*] who are the money representatives."

The code words served to invest the crude anti-Semitic agitation of the National Socialists with the dignity of political argument and economic analysis. Simultaneously they served to depict for the insiders the vast ramifications of the "Jewish conspiracy" and to document the multifarious roles of the mythic Jew. From the use of these code words, the insiders came to learn that all of Germany's enemies were Jews or tools of Jews.

## A QUESTION OF INTERPRETATION

Having defined the enemy exoterically and esoterically, Hitler in his speeches began to indicate how he would deal with that enemy. In those early days his favorite words were *"Entfernung"* and *"Aufräumung,"* both meaning "removal," "elimination," "cleaning up." (In *Mein Kampf* he preferred to use *"Beseitigung,"* also meaning "removal," "elimination," but less ambiguous about its finality.) . . .

"Removal" or "elimination" could be understood to mean "expulsion," and no doubt some of Hitler's listeners thought, if they thought at all about specifics, that he planned to drive the Jews out of Germany. . . .

The "either—or" that he had predicated in *Mein Kampf* was already evolving. In a speech on April 12, 1922, he said, referring to the "Jewish question": "Here, too, there can be no compromise—there are only two possibilities: either victory of the Aryan or annihilation of the Aryan and the victory of the Jew." Hitler frequently used the rhetorical device of paired antitheses. Strictly, the construction should have read:

> either victory of the Aryan [and annihilation of the Jew]
> or
> annihilation of the Aryan and the victory of the Jew.

The ellipsis of half of one pair was a signal to the cognoscenti of what he meant to say. . . .

## SUCCESSFUL COMMUNICATION

In the summer of 1922 a young man named Kurt Ludecke joined the National Socialist party and first met Hitler. Overwhelmed by both, he described his feelings at that time about the goals the movement had set for itself. These were his perceptions:

> The hugeness of the task and the absurdity of the hope swept over me. Its execution meant the liquidation of Jewry, of Rome, of liberalism with its tangled capitalistic connections; of Marxism, Bolshevism, Toryism—in short, an abrupt and complete break with the past and an assault on all existing world political forces.

Hitler's goals had unmistakably been communicated, despite the handicaps of esoteric language. Within the movement, the destruction of the Jews seemed to have been accepted as a basic programmatic task, though the average National Socialist probably still thought of pogrom, despite Hitler's frequently expressed opposition to such "emotional" outbursts of anti-Semitism. Still, even in those early days of the movement, when plans were being laid for the takeover of political power, the Jews figured importantly in Nazi strategy. The destruction of the Jews was not just a matter of words, in esoteric language even then, but a deathly reality. . . .

## THE CONNECTION BETWEEN RUSSIA AND THE JEWS

In retrospect, it seems likely that Hitler had settled on his radical "either—or" anti-Semitism already back in November 1918, as he claims in *Mein Kampf.* During the next few years Hitler's thinking remained geographically limited to Germany, albeit a "greater Germany." In his mind, the destruction of the Jews was the way to restore Germany to its virile Germandom. But once he encountered Alfred Rosenberg [an ethnic German who fled Russia after the Bolshevik Revolution and met Hitler in the early 1920s], Hitler's politi-

cal horizons expanded; he began to see the Jews primarily
as an international group whose destruction demanded an
international policy. . . .

Rosenberg further showed Hitler the possibilities of exploiting Russia as the political locus of international Jewry,
thus providing him with the eventual major theater of operations for his war against world Jewry. Under the influence
of Rosenberg and the other Russian and Ukrainian émigrés
with whom he associated and with whom the National Socialist movement collaborated, Russia became a key element
in Hitler's thinking. The émigrés spoke constantly of the im-
perative need to invade Russia so as to liberate it from the
bondage of the "Jew-Bolsheviks." In the very first issue of the
National Socialist newspaper *Völkischer Beobachter* [Racial
Observer], Rosenberg speculated that the Soviet Union would
shortly invade Poland and argued that Germany should then
intervene in what he called "the eastern marches of Germany." (Hitler was to use this idea in *Mein Kampf.*) Here, in
Rosenberg's mind, is the justification for Germany's "libera-
tion" of the Eastern territories from the "Jewish Bolsheviks,"
which would simultaneously restore the land to its original
German owner. It was an idea that Hitler and SS Commander
Heinrich Himmler were to hold tenaciously for the next
twenty years. Thus, fitting piece by piece into a large scheme,
Hitler combined the annihilation of the Jews with the destruction of Bolshevism, both of which could be accomplished by an invasion of Russia. The whole was supported
in racial terms: the innate racial perniciousness of the Jews
and the innate racial superiority of the Aryans whose culture
justified their need for Lebensraum. . . .

### SPEAKING PLAINLY IN *MEIN KAMPF*

Hitler wrote the first volume of *Mein Kampf* in Landsberg
prison in 1924 and the second volume in 1925, when he was
forbidden to engage in public speaking. The tone of the second is more aggressive and outspoken than that of the first;
Volume 2 is said to have benefited also from professional editorial assistance. The writing of *Mein Kampf* forced Hitler
into a process of organizing his ideas in one all-embracing
schema, however unsystematic and inchoate the final product. At its center was the war against the Jews that would
culminate in their annihilation and the world supremacy of
the Germans. The language, especially in the second vol-

ume, is no longer esoteric, but plainspoken. Though Hitler's hysteria and chiliastic rhetoric made the prose appear deceptively metaphorical, the words were meant to be taken literally. The destruction of the Jews is advocated time and again (all italics in original):

> *Only the elimination of the causes of our collapse, as well as the destruction of its beneficiaries, can create the premise for our outward fight for freedom.*

> . . . *It is the inexorable Jew who struggles for his domination over the nations.* No nation can remove this hand from its throat except by the sword. Only the assembled and concentrated might of a national passion rearing up in its strength can defy the international enslavement of peoples. Such a process is and remains a bloody one.

. . . Hitler kept projecting on the Jews the very destructive ideas he held about them: "The Jew would really devour the people of the earth, would become their master," "the international world Jew slowly but surely strangles us," "the Jew destroys the racial foundations of our existence and thus destroys our people for all time."

He even argued retroactively for a "preventive" war against the Jew in 1914–1918, which could have saved Germany from defeat:

> It would have been the duty of a serious government, now that the German worker had found his way back to his nation [in August 1914], to exterminate mercilessly the agitators who were misleading the nation.

> If the best men were dying at the front, the least we could do was to wipe out the vermin.

> If at the beginning of the War and during the War twelve or fifteen thousand of these Hebrew corrupters of the people had been held under poison gas . . . the sacrifice of millions at the front would not have been in vain. On the contrary: twelve thousand scoundrels eliminated in time might have saved the lives of a million real Germans, valuable for the future.

In the years between 1919 and 1925, the political climate had changed and Hitler now openly espoused his program of annihilation, without having to resort to concealment or camouflage. But only his followers took his words literally. Others, when they listened to Hitler or read *Mein Kampf*, dismissed his words as lunatic ravings. Yet these words were to become the blueprint for his policies when he came to power and would become, astonishingly, political and military reality.

## HITLER'S LONG-RANGE PLANS

Once Hitler adopted an ideological position, even a strategic one, he adhered to it with limpetlike fixity, fearful lest he be accused, if he changed his mind, of incertitude or capriciousness on "essential questions." He had long-range plans to realize his ideological goals, and the destruction of the Jews was at their center.

The grand design was in his head. He did not spell it out in concrete strategy. Nothing was written down. . . . He even elevated his tactics of secrecy into a strategic principle: as few people as possible to know as little as possible as late as possible.

The implementation of his plans was contingent on the opportunism of the moment or the expediency of delay. As head of both the German state and the National Socialist movement, he had to weigh the urgent passions of the little man in the party against the foreign-policy interests of the state, and to balance his own desire for surprise attack with the state's readiness to mount one. Often he decided suddenly that the opportune occasion had arrived to carry out a specific aspect of his program, and then the practical work had quickly to be improvised.

In Hitler's schema, the removal of the Jews from posts in the state apparatus and from society's cultural and educational institutions represented, along with the remilitarization of Germany, the first phase of his program, the internal cleansing and healing of Germany. Whereas the anti-Jewish legislation of 1933 was for him merely the prerequisite for later stages of his program that would culminate in the Final Solution, this undoing of the emancipation of the German Jews represented for the conventional anti-Semites the attainment of their political ambitions. That was the time when the widest consensus existed in Germany with regard to anti-Semitism, when the values and goals of the conventional anti-Semites were identical and undistinguishable from those of the radical anti-Semites. That particular convergence made it easier for the conventional anti-Semites subsequently to acquiesce to the radical anti-Semitic program.

## ANTI-JEWISH LAWS

At the National Socialist party congress in Nuremberg in September 1935, Hitler introduced new anti-Jewish legislation, describing these laws as a repayment of a debt of gratitude to the National Socialist party, under whose aegis Germany had regained her freedom, and as the fulfillment of an important plank of the movement's program. The Reich Citizenship Law, depriving the German Jews of the rights and protections of citizenship, marked the goal of conventional anti-Semitism—the total disenfranchisement of the Jews.

### HISTORICAL EXAMPLES OF MASS MURDER

*James Pool is the author of* Who Financed Hitler? *and* Hitler and His Secret Partners: Contributions, Loot, and Rewards. *In the following excerpt, Pool points out that Hitler modeled the Holocaust on prior attempts at genocide, including the near-extermination of the American Indians.*

Hitler did not approach the problem of extermination of the Jews haphazardly. He had carefully studied some of the most prominent examples of mass murder in history. . . .

Hitler aspired to be a modern-day Genghis Khan. He had carefully studied the ancient migrations and destructions of peoples. His morality was that of the Dark Ages combined with a Darwinist survival-of-the-fittest philosophy. "Natural instincts," he once told one of his associates, "bid all living beings not merely to conquer their enemies, but also to destroy them. In ancient times it was the victor's prerogative to destroy entire tribes, entire peoples.". . .

Hitler drew another example of mass murder from American history. Since his youth he had been obsessed with the Wild West stories of Karl May. He viewed the fighting between cowboys and Indians in racial terms. In many of his speeches he referred with admiration to the victory of the white race in settling the American continent and driving out the inferior peoples, the Indians. With great fascination he listened to stories, which some of his associates who had been in America told him about the massacres of the Indians by the U.S. Cavalry.

He was very interested in the way the Indian population had rapidly declined due to epidemics and starvation when the United States government forced them to live on the reservations. He thought the American government's forced migrations of the Indians over great distances to barren reservation land was a deliberate policy of extermination. Just how much Hitler took from the American example of the destruction of the Indian nations for his plans of the Holocaust is hard to say; however, frightening parallels can be drawn.

James Pool, *Hitler and His Secret Partners: Contributions, Loot, and Rewards,* 1997.

The Law for the Protection of German Blood and German Honor, on the other hand, even though it drew heavily upon a half-century's tradition of racist anti-Semitism, was a new departure. With its implementing decrees and with those of the Reich Citizenship Law, it initiated Hitler's program of radical anti-Semitism, with the process of identifying and isolating the Jews from the non-Jews, readying them, as it were, for their later fate.

The Nuremberg Laws were a watershed also in another respect, to which Hitler alluded ominously. In introducing the Law for the Protection of German Blood and German Honor, he said that it was "an attempt to regulate by law a problem which, in the event of repeated failure, would have to be transferred by law to the National Socialist party for final solution." He was, it now appears, indicating that the state had come to the end of its competency in handling the Jewish question and that thenceforth all anti-Jewish measures would be carried out by the party. In this period, too, he spoke of sweeping plans for the Jews, involving ghettos and possibly a reservation, and on another occasion he talked of carrying out the "euthanasia" murder program once war came.

## PREPARING FOR THE SECOND PHASE

By the summer of 1936, Hitler believed that the first phase of his program—the internal domestic stage—was virtually completed and in August, having composed a memorandum on the Four Year Plan, he entered into preparations for the second phase—aggression and war. That memorandum, with its ideological justification for a war against "Jewish Bolshevism," transformed *Mein Kampf* into state policy. The doctrine of the party leader now became the plan for the state. . . .

Hitler appointed Hermann Göring to be his Plenipotentiary for the Four Year Plan and gave him a copy of that memorandum. They surely discussed aspects of this program, and Hitler must have shared his plans concerning the Jews. At least one other person also shared Hitler's confidences in this respect at this time—Heinrich Himmler. In the early summer of 1936 Himmler had, with Hitler's support, become Reichsführer-SS and Chief of the German Police, directly subordinate to Hitler and only to him. Hitler had by then already decided to hand over to the National Socialist movement the authority to "solve" the Jewish question. Himmler, then one of the most powerful figures in the party, had probably been inducted into the inmost circle and told of Hitler's plans for war and the destruction of the Jews—a task that would fall, at the proper time, within his jurisdiction. . . .

## INSTIGATING THE FINAL SOLUTION

On January 30, 1939, Hitler made his declaration of war against the Jews, promising "the destruction of the Jewish race in Europe." The decision to proceed with this irreversible mission had already been taken. Thenceforth the Final Solution entered the stage of practical planning for implementation. Hitler's first opportunity to put into practice his ideas about killing the crippled and insane presented itself at this time, and shortly thereafter, on April 3, 1939, he instructed General Wilhelm Keitel to start planning the invasion of Poland.

Hitler's gamble, then, was on a quick military victory in Poland, to be completed before Russia could gather wits or forces to act. Afterward he would consolidate his position, using Poland as the launching pad for his invasion of Russia. (The rapprochement with Russia, ideologically embarrassing but tactically expedient, did not at all affect his long-range plans, but merely eased his short-range military risks.) While planning the Polish invasion, Hitler, Himmler, and SS General Reinhard Heydrich worked out the first stage of the Final Solution, concentrating the Jews while consolidating the Polish gains. Heydrich's instructions to the chiefs of the Einsatzgruppen [special killing groups] on September 21, 1939, are clear enough about present program and future intentions. The second, ultimate stage of the Final Solution was to be synchronized with the attack on Russia, when "Jewish Bolshevism" would be destroyed. . . .

In December 1940 Operation Barbarossa [the German invasion of Russia] entered the formal planning stage, and Hitler then no doubt explored with Himmler, and perhaps Heydrich, various practical possibilities for the last stage of the Final Solution. By February 1941 they had decided on a two-pronged attack against the Jews. In the active war zone, the Einsatzgruppen would coordinate their murder attack on the Jews with the military invasion. The rest of the European Jews in countries under German occupation or governed by rulers sympathetic to Germany would be brought to annihilation camps in or near the Generalgouvernement of Poland. . . . All the decisions had been taken. The rest was a matter of technology, administrative clearance, and efficient operation. Through a maze of time Hitler's decision of November 1918 led to Operation Barbarossa. There never had been any ideological deviation or wavering determination. In the end only the question of opportunity mattered.

The Final Solution grew out of a matrix formed by traditional anti-Semitism, the paranoid delusions that seized Germany after World War I, and the emergence of Hitler and the National Socialist movement. Without Hitler, the charismatic political leader, who believed he had a mission to annihilate the Jews, the Final Solution would not have occurred.

## CHAPTER 4

# The Historical Significance of Adolf Hitler

# The Global Impact of Hitler's War

Norman Rich

Although Adolf Hitler did not achieve his goal of global domination, the Second World War had a profound impact on the world on several different levels, Norman Rich reveals. First, he writes, the war shattered the dominance of the great powers of Western Europe and enabled the Soviet Union and the United States to emerge as two giant superpowers. The war also exposed some uncomfortable truths about human nature, Rich asserts, such as the lasting appeal of dictatorial rule and racist nationalism. He explains that many nationalistic groups in countries throughout the world still promote racist ideology and brutal acts of genocide similar to those practiced by Hitler's Nazis. Rich is a retired professor of history at Brown University in Providence, Rhode Island. He is the author of several books, including *Hitler's War Aims*, from which the following selection is taken.

In making a final assessment of Adolf Hitler's war aims, it is important to bear in mind that the Nazi dictator was never an entirely free agent, that his aims were constantly affected by changes in Germany's political and military situation, and that his ambition expanded as new opportunities opened before him. Thus, although he professed not to be interested in the acquisition of overseas colonies, he did not hesitate to lay claim to an immense colonial empire in central Africa when it seemed likely that he would soon be able to acquire one. As Hitler never controlled this part of Africa, or the majority of other overseas territories coveted by German colonial enthusiasts, the ultimate extent of his colonial ambitions must remain a matter of speculation.

Excerpted from *Hitler's War Aims: The Establishment of the New Order*, by Norman Rich. Copyright ©1974 by W.W. Norton and Company, Inc. Reprinted by permission of W.W. Norton and Company, Inc.

It was different with Europe, however, where Hitler's actual policies, viewed in conjunction with his policy statements, guidelines, and directives, give a very clear indication of his intentions. These policies demonstrate beyond all doubt that through all the vicissitudes of his career Hitler adhered with fanatic consistency to the two central objectives of his ideological program: the purification of the Germanic race through the removal of all non-Aryan racial elements; and the conquest of *Lebensraum* [living space] in Eastern Europe to ensure the security of the Germanic race for all time. . . .

## THE SHATTERING EFFECTS OF WORLD WAR II

Germany, however, did not win the war, and by 1945 Hitler's dream of empire, and with it Germany and a great part of Europe, lay in ruins. After the First World War the great powers of Europe, although weakened in terms of manpower and resources, had remained world powers. Aided by the withdrawal of the United States and the Soviet Union into isolationism, they had continued to make many of the major policy decisions affecting the world at large. It was Hitler's war which brought to an end the age of European global primacy, which placed a great part of Central and Eastern Europe under Soviet dominion, and which left the states of Western Europe perilously lodged between the millstones of Russian/Asiatic power in the east and American power in the west.

Apart from altering the power structure of the world, the Nazi catastrophe shattered whatever illusions men may have held about the moral progress of humankind, starkly revealing how thin was the veneer of humanitarian civilization in the modern world, even in countries which took great pride in their cultural achievements. More sinister still, the Nazis demonstrated how easy it is for man to find rational, even idealistic and moral, motives to carry out inhuman actions. . . .

The Nazis demonstrated further that, despite two centuries of democratic revolution and presumed political enlightenment in Europe, authoritarianism was by no means discredited as a form of government, for there were people in every part of Europe who had actually welcomed dictatorial rule as a means of solving the increasingly complex problems of industrial society. It would appear, moreover, that industrialization in itself had made it easier to impose and maintain an authoritarian regime, at least over the short run. The Nazis, at all events, seem to have had least difficulty controlling societies with a relatively high degree of industrial and technological development, whose predominantly urban populations were dependent for their very existence on the proper functioning of their industrial and technological apparatus. By contrast, the Nazis had somewhat greater difficulty controlling predominantly rural societies, whose populations were more scattered and had more direct access to the basic necessities of life. . . .

## THE PERSISTENT APPEAL OF RACIST NATIONALISM

The most disturbing consideration of all, in the light of the Nazi experience, is the innate appeal of Nazism itself, not necessarily Nazism labeled as such, but the cult of racial nationalism which was the basic ingredient of the Nazi doctrine. On every continent we still find racial nationalist movements marshaled under the familiar slogans of national freedom and self-determination, sovereignty and independence—the very slogans which Nazism exploited so successfully. And in many cases these movements have been accompanied by programs of genocide, the compulsory relocation of entire racial or national communities, and acts of brutality that stun the imagination. Apart from the irrational passions and prejudices involved in all national-racial policies, or the even more incalculable factors of stupidity, panic, or sheer momentum, the common denominator of all of them appears to be a search for security, whether the government of a particular society be fascist, communist, or democratic. It remains one of the great misfortunes of mankind that this search is still so frequently conducted on the basis of the same simplistic logic that characterized the policies of Hitler, and that so many national-racial groups continue to seek the temporal salvation of their species of humanity at the risk of its dehumanization.

The basic fallacy in all such programs, as it was in Hitler's, is the belief that the racial-national community is somehow ordained by natural law to be the fundamental unit of human society, and the concomitant belief that once it achieves an adequate economic base and all domestic and external threats on the part of alien races and nations have been eliminated, the security of that community will be assured. Yet it is only necessary to look at the record of any national state, no matter how prosperous, powerful, or racially homogeneous, to realize how erroneous these assumptions are. For national states, like all human organizations, inevitably breed personal and political rivalries, class and social tensions, and other forces that are a constant threat to social stability and security. Perhaps an absolutely regimented totalitarian regime may some day resolve such problems through drugs or programs of brain surgery, but again it would be a matter of offering a nation security at the expense of its humanity.

In the case of the Nazis, it is one of the great ironies of his-

## THE REPERCUSSIONS OF "HITLER'S WAR"

*Jeremy Noakes teaches history at the University of Exeter in England. In the following excerpt, he recounts the worldwide impact of the Second World War and the Holocaust.*

The results of 'Hitler's War' are all around us today: the emergence of the United States and the Soviet Union as 'superpowers' and the division of Europe into spheres of influence between them; the effective colonisation of eastern Europe by the Soviet Union; the loss of one-third of German territory and the division of the rest into two separate German states; the destruction of the pre-war settlement in the Middle East and the creation of some of the problems in that area which still plague us today; and the drastic acceleration in the process of decolonisation outside Europe provoked by the war. . . . Indeed, more generally, the main effect of the war was to accelerate change—political, economic, social and technological change—in all those countries involved in it and in many that were not, perhaps most notably the development of nuclear weapons many years earlier than would otherwise have happened, with all its repercussions for post-war international relations. But, of course, the impact of Hitler and of Nazi Germany on the rest of the world was not felt solely in terms of the effect of the Second World War. The appalling atrocities committed in the concentration camps and, in particular, the Jewish holocaust were not only catastrophic events in themselves, but the fact that they were perpetrated by one of the most culturally sophisticated nations raised grave doubts about the vulnerability of Western culture, doubts which have continued to trouble the second half of the twentieth century.

Jeremy Noakes, *History Today*, 1980.

tory (and one of the few examples of the justice of fate in the historical process) that Hitler's racial policies, which were supposed to provide the foundation of German national security, doomed the Nazi racial state from the start. For non-Aryan scientists driven from Hitler's Europe played a major role in the development of weapons which made an ultimate German victory impossible.

## No Real Security

Even if Hitler had emerged triumphant from the Second World War, however, the entire history of the Nazi movement suggests that his fundamental war aim—security for the German people—would have eluded him. There was never any assurance that the Aryan race, or that mélange of nationalities Hitler defined as Aryan, would have held together over the long or even the short run to form a stable society. Hitler himself constantly spoke of the possibility of his assassination and realized that his own person was at no time secure. This same lack of security would even more have been the lot of his successors and their lieutenants.

As for the masses of the German people, what kind of security did Hitler in fact give them? The security to serve in his organizations from the cradle to the grave; the security to be under the permanent surveillance of state and party authorities, to be spied on by neighbors and colleagues; the security of the gibbet or the concentration camp if they deviated, or were suspected of deviating, from official orthodoxy; the security to be maimed or killed in the wars Hitler fought in the name of national security, and which he believed would have to be waged in the future to preserve the security already achieved.

## Hitler's Terrible Lesson

A totalitarian form of security can appeal to intelligent and idealistic people, those who yearn for Utopia and believe it can be attained by the logical and ruthless application of scientific or ideological principles to the problems of human society. But above all such security appeals to the perennial conformists who find security in regulations and orders, in having no need to make decisions or judgments of their own. Yet by any standard this remains a precarious and sterile security, a regimentation of the minds and bodies of men which, in the Nazi experience at least, throttled the very cultural creativity which Hitler had declared to be the primary objective of his New Order. In the end, one of the saddest features of the Nazi experience is that out of all the suffering, the bloodshed, and the destruction which Nazism inflicted on the world, the Nazi movement contributed nothing whatever to human culture and civilization. Nothing except a terrible lesson about how fragile and vulnerable human civilization is.

# Hitler's Devastating Legacy to Germany

Ian Kershaw

Ian Kershaw is a professor of modern history at the University of Sheffield in Great Britain. He is the author of *The "Hitler Myth": Image and Reality in the Third Reich* and *Hitler, 1889–1936: Hubris* (the first volume of a projected two-volume set). The following excerpt is taken from Kershaw's book *Hitler*, a short analysis of Hitler's life and power. Kershaw discusses different aspects of Hitler's legacy to the German nation, none of which are positive. According to Kershaw, Hitler contributed nothing of lasting value to Germany: His plans that may have benefitted German society never went into effect, while in other areas his policies stifled economic growth and cultural freedom. Furthermore, the author relates that when Hitler realized the war was lost, he attempted to destroy the German army and even Germany itself. Hitler then committed suicide, leaving the German people to bear the burden of his destructive acts, Kershaw concludes.

The hallmark of Adolf Hitler's power was destruction. His political 'career' began out of the destruction of the Germany he had until then identified with, 'destroyed' in his mind by the 'Marxist' [communist] revolution of 1918. It ended in the far more comprehensive destruction of 'his' Germany through total defeat and devastation in 1945. Twelve years of his rule destroyed 'old' Germany, both territorially and in terms of its social order. They also destroyed 'old' Europe, both physically and in terms of its political order.

From the beginning, Hitler's most powerful driving force was a destructive one. The word 'annihilation' (*Vernichtung*) was seldom far from his lips, from his earliest speeches in

Munich beerhalls down to his apocalyptic visions in the East Prussian Führer Headquarters and in the Berlin bunker. . . .

## HITLER ALMOST DESTROYED GERMANY

Hitler's destructive drive did not spare his own army. The staggering losses at the front left him totally unmoved. The only time he was accidentally confronted with wounded soldiers in a train standing next to the Führer train, he had the curtains of his carriage drawn. When his own strategic decisions left the German Sixth Army encircled at Stalingrad, he refused to consider a break-out and condemned them to their destruction. His reaction to the catastrophe was incomprehension at Field Marshal Friedrich Paulus's choice of surrender rather than death.

In 1944 Hitler rested his hope not on building a fighter defence formation capable of heading off enemy bombers, but on reducing English cities to rubble through the V-weapons [advanced bombs and rockets the Germans were trying to develop]. If the atom bomb had been available, there is no doubt whatsoever that he would have used it against London. As it was, German cities were increasingly reduced to ashes. Hitler never visited a single one, never showed signs of sympathy for the bombed-out populations, never revealed any remorse for the suffering inflicted upon German families. His reactions were invariably paroxysms of fury at the ineptitude of the Luftwaffe [air force] to defend Germany, and vows to avenge the destruction by wreaking even greater destruction on British cities.

In the end, true to his own principles, Hitler tried to destroy Germany's chances of surviving him, through his . . . scorched-earth commands of 1945. The German people had, in his eyes, deserved their own destruction since they had not proved strong enough to destroy the arch-enemy of Bolshevism [communism].

## NO POSITIVE LEGACY

In this catalogue of destruction, there is nothing which stands as a positive legacy of the years of Hitler's power. In art, architecture, music and literature, the Hitler regime stifled innovation and originality. Creative art, writing and thinking largely went into exile along with the representatives of 'decadent' art or forbidden literature. The loss to German culture through the forced emigration of writers of the calibre of

Thomas and Heinrich Mann, Arnold and Stefan Zweig, Alfred Döblin and Bertold Brecht, the artists Wassily Kandinsky, Paul Klee and Oskar Kokoschka, and the architects Walter Gropius and Ludwig Mies van der Rohe was incalculable. Artists like Emil Nolde and writers like Gottfried Benn, who began with high hopes of the Third Reich, found themselves rapidly disillusioned and entered a form of 'inner emigration,' their works banned or their creativity ended for the duration of Nazi rule. In the field of music, the late compositions of Richard Strauss, the *Carmina Burana* of Carl Orff, and the continued presence of the leading conductor Wilhelm Furtwängler formed only partial compensation for the loss of Arnold Schönberg and Paul Hindemith, and the banning of the music of [Jewish composers] Felix Mendelssohn and Gustav Mahler. Nazism was incapable of filling the vacuum left by its cultural blood-letting. Culturally, the Third Reich amounted to twelve sterile years.

Nor in the spheres of politics and economics did the Hitler era produce anything of lasting value. No governmental form or system which could serve as a possible model emerged. Lack of system, and lack of structure, in fact, were the characteristics of the Hitler state. Destruction of coherent channels of governmental authority rather than the erection of a definable 'system' of authoritarian administration was the prevailing feature. In economics, too, Hitler's regime left only negative lessons for the future. 'Nazi economics' were utterly predatory in nature, devoid of potential as a durable 'system'. They were based upon the idea of a modern form of slavery within state-directed capitalism—symbolised above all by the huge industrial complex at Auschwitz, in which the slave labour of major German firms was worked to death or liquidated when no longer capable of work. The in-built contradictions scarcely provided a recipe for a lasting economic 'new order'. It is hardly any wonder that already by the middle of the war, conceptions of a more rational economic order in which Nazi ideals played no part were being confidentially discussed in business circles.

## PLANS THAT NEVER SAW FRUITION

Is the negative legacy of Nazism, its lack of constructive capacity, simply a consequence of Germany's total defeat? Have we underrated the capability of the Hitler regime to develop into a lasting system of power had the war been won?

Clearly, all Nazi plans for the future were predicated upon final victory being achieved. Grandiose architectural plans, in which Hitler took the keenest interest—he was still working on the plan for remodelling Linz with the Red Army at the gates of Berlin—were elaborated for the rebuilding of German cities on a monumental scale. Hitler also had visions . . . of a future highly advanced industrialised and technologically developed society, for which the conquered areas would provide raw materials and suppressed racial inferiors the labour. Capitalist industry would fall in line, or be taken over by the state if it could thereby be run more effectively. German workers would replace an effete bourgeoisie as a politically qualified elite. The vision was that of a revolutionary transformation of German society. Meanwhile, Robert Ley—Labour Front boss and from 1941 Housing Commissar—was masterminding future schemes for the wholesale reconstruction of social insurance provision . . . and for huge housing programmes. None of this came remotely near to fruition. More dwellings disappeared under the hail of bombs than could possibly have been built under Ley's ambitious housing programme. And the post-war West German social insurance programme drew on antecedents in imperial and Weimar Germany, but not on the model of the Third Reich.

Only a successful outcome to the war could have enabled the Nazi vision of a new society to be realised. Hitler is reported as having said, in the last weeks of the Third Reich, that he needed twenty years to produce an elite which had drunk his ideals like milk from the mother's breast. But, he added, the problem had been that time had always been against Germany. . . .

Devoid of constructive, creative energy, articulating only ever wilder urges to destroy, the likeliest end to Hitler's power was, then, the end which did eventually take place: a bullet in the head, leaving the German people to pay the price for their readiness to be taken in by a leader offering not limited policy options, but a tempting, though illusory and empty, chiliastic vision of political redemption.

# Images of Hitler in Popular Culture

Alvin H. Rosenfeld

In the following reading, Alvin H. Rosenfeld explores
the use of imagery related to Hitler and the Nazis in
novels, movies, TV shows, music, and other facets of
modern popular culture. He shows how the images
of Hitler presented in these works frequently have
little to do with the historical Hitler, especially since
they tend to minimize or ignore his role in the Holocaust. Such sanitizing—and even glorifying—of
Hitler can be dangerous, Rosenfeld warns. At a time
when neo-Nazi revisionists are arguing that the
Holocaust never happened, he writes, it is essential
to always keep in mind Hitler's true historical significance. Rosenfeld acknowledges that people will remain fascinated by Hitler, but he cautions that the
type of evil Hitler represents is extremely dangerous
and should not be taken lightly. Rosenfeld is the
chairman of the Jewish Studies Department at Indiana University in Bloomington and the author of
*Imagining Hitler*, from which the following reading
is excerpted.

The long-legged, high-kicking beauties in Mel Brooks's *The
Producers* look like any other chorus line of dancers but for a
single exception: they are suited out in the black uniforms of
the SS. The dance they perform, backed by a second chorus
line of Valkyries, is called "Springtime for Hitler" and is
meant to be a musical burlesque of Nazi antics. The number
mixes mock-politics with female flesh, high-spirited farce
with showy extravaganza. It finds a parallel in Brooks's film,
*To Be or Not to Be*, in a bizarre song-and-dance routine called
"Naughty Nazis." In both cases, one looks on and laughs.

A skit on the popular television show *Saturday Night Live*

Excerpted from *Imagining Hitler*, by Alvin H. Rosenfeld. Copyright ©1985 by Alvin H.
Rosenfeld. Reprinted by permission of the publisher, Indiana University Press.

portrays Adolf Hitler and Eva Braun fumbling over one an-other like two clumsy teenagers in heat. It's silly and stupid but probably just funny enough to get a laugh. Not so *The National Lampoon* Hitler jokes, which are neither naughty nor funny but mostly just vulgar, tasteless, sick. Neverthe-less, they continue to appear, so someone must like them. Is it the same crowd that listens to the popular singer David Bowie croon about "visions of swastikas in my head," that snaps up the premier number of Larry Flynt's magazine *The Rebel* because it features a huge swastika on its cover, that likes wearing punk styles that use Nazi symbols as fashion-able emblems of a new social defiance?

## NAZI SYMBOLS AND POP CULTURE

One could multiply these examples many times over, but that would only belabor the obvious: the signs and symbols of the Third Reich have become part of the common lan-guage of popular culture and are today all around us. In En-gland, according to the Alternative Holiday Catalogue, one can even "vacation" in a Nazi-style camp, "complete with barbed wire, searchlights, watch towers, and fifty guards in SS uniforms." This idea of an Auschwitz–as–theme park has not yet crossed over to this side of the Atlantic, but there is still plenty of opportunity for those who want to fantasize about the "naughty Nazis." You can giggle over the Nazi buf-foons of popular television shows, flaunt the swastika as your personal badge of disaffection, ogle the girls in the high black boots. For the children, there is *When Hitler Stole Pink Rabbit* and such "simulation games" as "Gestapo: A Learn-ing Experience about the Holocaust."

In sum, Hitler has become a gag, an adornment, a piece of the fun. If one cannot yet talk about the arrival of a Nazi chic, one can say that it is easy—and in no way regarded as a sign of gross social deviance—to indulge a taste for the stylistic gestures of a latter-day pop fascism, although a fascism com-monly regarded as being without political implications. As the owner of a London boutique for punk fashions explains, "They like the Nazi things because they are interesting dec-orations." Is it possible that it never crossed the lady's mind that "the Nazi things" have a history of some consequence behind them?

It is possible. A prolonged dalliance with Nazi-inspired fun-and-games—with countless jokes, fads, films, fictionalizations: the whole run of popular and pornographic indul-gences—not only dulls political awareness but dissipates and ultimately defeats the historical sense. Laugh at Hitler often enough, dress him up as a stage villain, convert him into a cartoon of frightful or ridiculous demeanor, and in time you will no longer know who or what he was. Play with the symbols of his Reich as if they were harmless toys and before long the distractions of mind generated by the plea-sures of lighthearted amusement weaken the sanctions of historical memory. "Holocaust" then comes to mind more readily as a popular television show than as an unprece-dented crime within history. As for Hitler, rendered com-monplace, he becomes a conventional focus of the leisure and entertainment industries, even something of a pop hero. According to David Bowie, Hitler was "one of the first rock stars." To catch him in a musical setting, you can, if you wish, listen to some of the songs of "Pink Floyd" or tune in to the English rock opera *Der Führer* and hear Eva Braun sing, in a voice of moony enchantment, "When I'm leaning against his shoulder, the bad times are over."

## BEGINNING TO FORGET?

With such goings-on as these, the bad times may be only just beginning. While probably none of what has been described above is specifically intended as "pro-Nazi," its inevitable ef-fect is to undermine any sane vision of culture and ulti-mately to erase the fingerprints of Hitler from a history of mass murder. To popularize the man and his crimes is to trivialize them and, in time, to render them almost invisible. Here, in the words of Saul Friedländer, is one prominent ex-ample of that process:

> A few months ago I saw Joachim Fest's film, *Hitler: A Career*, in a movie theater in Munich. The dazzling rise, the titanic energy, the Luciferian fall: it is all there. As for the extermi-nation of the Jews, a few words in passing, no more. An in-consequential shadow of this grandiose tableau. For anyone who does not know the facts, the power and the glory still re-main, followed by a veritable vengeance of the gods. . . .

> For anyone who does not know the facts, the mystical com-munion with the brownshirt revolution and its martyrs still remains.

> Thus is evidence transformed over the years, thus do memo-ries crumble away.

The role of art in the erosion, as well as the establishment, of historical memory is fundamental, for most people do not have a primary relationship to "the facts" and learn about them secondhand, through the mediations of word and image. With few exceptions, we "see" what we are given to see, "know" what we are given to know, and thus come to retain in memory what impresses itself on us as vision and knowledge. We owe to the Czech writer Milan Kundera the insight that such knowledge has the deepest political consequences, indeed that "the struggle of man against power is the struggle of memory against forgetting." One can, in this sense, talk about art's implication in a politics of remembrance as well as a politics of forgetting, an implication not lost on any writer who sifts through the debris of history in an effort to reconstruct the past or on any national leader who is alert to the legendary or mythic dimensions of the past and has the gift of reviving them for his own political objectives. In both cases, the refashioning of the past need not be determined by any special fidelity to history, as if the latter has been fixed once and for all and is no longer malleable to the pressures of mind or imagination; rather, the appeal to the past follows the course of feeling—of dream, impulse, hope, or wish—and makes of the "facts" new fictions of desire.

## WHITEWASHING HISTORY

What happens to our sense of reality as a consequence of these developments is obvious to any reader of contemporary fiction or any observer of contemporary politics. As the novelist E.L. Doctorow put it a while back, "There is no longer any such thing as fiction or non-fiction; there's only narrative." In the words of the same author: "What's real and what isn't—I used to know, but I've forgotten." William Styron carries this line of thinking beyond Doctorow's playful agnosticism to his own more deeply felt historical relativism:

> Facts *per se* are preposterous. They are like the fuzz that collects in the top of dirty closets. They don't really mean anything. . . . A novelist dealing with history has to be able to say that such and such a fact is totally irrelevant, and to Hell with the person who insists that it has any real, utmost relevance. . . . Certain facts . . . can be dispensed with out of hand, because to yield to them would be to yield or to compromise the novelist's own aesthetic honesty. . . . A brute, an idiotic preoccupation with crude fact is death to a novel, and death to the novelist.

Styron's desires as a novelist—or the imperatives of what he calls his "own aesthetic honesty"—brought him, in writing *Sophie's Choice*, to refashion Hans Frank, the Nazi Governor General of a large part of occupied Poland, as a Jew, and to make Rudolf Höss, the Commandant of Auschwitz, seem almost a decent man. . . . In his film, *Zelig*, Woody Allen uses a fake Oswald Pohl, the head of the SS Economic-Administrative Main Office and, as such, the person chiefly responsible for the concentration camp business, to comment in pseudohistorical terms on a fictitious character that Pohl allegedly "knew" in Nazi Germany. As in every one of these instances, it is a characteristic of the new narrative modes that distinctions between what is real and what is imagined drop away: historical figures take on fictional dimensions, fictional characters are placed within historical settings, and there is an intermingling of illusion and historically accredited reality. . . . To what degree can an author play with, reshape, or distort our sense of the past without doing damage to our overall sense of reality? When, as has been the case, critics call *Sophie's Choice* a "brilliant historical novel," are we not approaching a point of epistemological risk, at which our ability to know the difference between historical fiction and fictitious history begins to diminish and, for some, may begin to disappear?

These questions are not new and could be asked as well about works of literature that date back as far as Shakespeare's history plays and the fiction of Sir Walter Scott and Leo Tolstoy, but in recent years they have assumed a greater degree of seriousness and even taken on a certain urgency. They have done so at a time when "reality" itself has become a more extreme and elusive concept, when our ability to represent it within language has been called into question, and when the political will to misrepresent has become blatant and unrestrained. The aesthetic issues that always attend questions of representation take on a new edge when what is being represented is Hitler and Hitlerism, all the more so at a time when the Nazi Holocaust of the Jews is regularly labeled a "hoax" by the revisionists and their allies. . . .

## THE LASTING CULTURAL POWER OF HITLER

From all one can see, Hitler is not about to be demobilized soon. In politics and in literature—and as they relate to Hitler there is the temptation for the two to merge and become almost one—all the signs indicate a flourishing career ahead. William Gass, one of our most imaginatively resourceful writers, is at work on a novel that invokes Hitler to explore what he calls a "fascism of the heart." The pornographers will continue to appeal to their own version of this fascination (a fascism of the loins?) by turning out formulaic fiction that links eroticism with Nazism. . . . No doubt there will be television replays of *Holocaust, The Last Days of Hitler, The Winds of War, The Bunker, Blood and Honor*—all of which succeed in keeping images of the Third Reich steadily before the viewing public. *The National Lampoon* will recycle more of its Hitler jokes, the *National Examiner* will report sensational new sightings of fugitive Nazis, the revisionists will announce new "evidence" that the Holocaust never happened.

It is predictable that a rock group will emerge that will outdo all others in raucous exhibitionism of Nazi sentiment and paraphernalia and that new New-Style boutiques will highlight Storm-Trooper uniforms for men and something equally brutal for women as the latest craze in fashion. As of this writing, the newest and raciest clothing item in London's Petticoat Lane are Hitler T-shirts, which feature a picture of the Führer under the heading "European Tour 1939–1945." The "tour" commences with "September 1939—Poland" and concludes with "July 1945—Berlin Bunker." For a change-off, one can also pick up black T-shirts at the stalls emblazoned with the word "Bundeswehr" [German military].

For years hobby shops have registered steady sales in model replicas of World War II German tanks and planes—cheaper ones for the children, more expensive ones for their elders. As part of this same market, but on a more serious and higher-priced level, there will continue to be a brisk collector's trade in original Nazi insignia, swords, and other symbols of the Reich, as there will be in oversized picture books on World War II weapons and warfare. Richly illustrated "lives" of Hitler will appear, as will expensive, coffee-table albums of concentration camp photographs and artwork. Someone will turn up long-lost Hitler watercolors, medical records, astrological charts, automobiles—anything that Hitler may have touched or been touched by. . . . What is at stake here, then, is not historical credibility but narrativity—stories, emblems, and images that will fascinate and compel.

## FASCINATION WITH EVIL

True, much of what has just been described is in the realm of kitsch and quatsch—the detritus of history refashioned into cheap and unworthy artifice—but it was at least partly on the rivers of such junk that Hitler originally floated into power and remains afloat still today. It is not high scholarship or high art, let alone high ideals, that sustains him but something a good deal further down in consciousness and culture. Call it the blood lusts of primitive instinct or the anarchic and nihilistic impulses that want to be satisfied free of all restraints. Or call it, as Hitler himself called it, the mad ambition of "Weltmacht oder Niedergang"—"world power or ruin." Whatever else he may exemplify, Hitler stands for, appeals to, and calls forth an unprecedented extremity of destructive will. Charles Hamilton, the New York autograph dealer, probably summed up as well as anyone the secret of Hitler's posthumous appeal when, in considering the value of an object alleged to be Hitler's skull, he said simply, "Hitler is the supreme criminal of all times. He out-Neroes Nero, he out-Caligulas Caligula. Therefore, he is a most fascinating man."

It is easy to exploit a figure that generates such fascination, far less easy to contain the damage it may do once it is released into the world. The fate of symbols is always unpredictable, all the more so when they have behind them as much turbulence and unmastered energy as those that attach to Hitler. One recalls in this context an insight of Elias Canetti, whose notebook jottings of 1942 include the following entry: "Some sentences release their poison only years after." Whether Canetti had been listening to one of Hitler's speeches when he wrote these words is unknown, but one readily sees how they could apply to the rhetoric of the Third Reich and how they might apply as well today, when the words and images of that era have assumed such popular currency. To be sure, they circulate now in another mood and in a different, less dangerous political climate. All the same, there is inherent in the image of Nazism a venom that, once released onto the page and into the mind, has the potential to turn lethal. As imaginative life domesticates images of Hitler and political life continues to exploit him, one should not be surprised to see the old poison once more begin to flow free.

Just where it will go and what damage it may do is anybody's guess. Most of those involved in popularizing Hitler are probably too busy making money and having fun to give any thought to the social and political consequences of their efforts. As for the others, who deliberately set about manipulating historical symbols, the consequences have no doubt been far more precisely calculated by them. In both cases, the appeal to the Third Reich, whether for reasons of commercial or political profit, means a perpetuation in image of the very worst that history has given us and a revivification of the prospect that it may come round once again.

## HITLER'S GHOST

One would rather be rid of the Nazi nightmare once and for all, but it has become too deeply embedded in fantasy life to be quickly or easily denied. The extensions, distortions, and various exploitations of Nazi symbolism have by now become part of the history of the Nazi era as it has penetrated contemporary consciousness. In this respect, Hitler has won, for he knew better than most that if truth has its appeal, so, too, do certain lies, which are every bit as irrepressible once they catch hold. How they have come to catch hold should by now be clear. For years the image of the man and his times has been broadly and successfully projected through the work of novelists, filmmakers, and other fictioneers, and it is they who have assumed and directed the narrative destiny of the Nazi period. Consequently, set loose by a hundred different stories, legends, and myths, the ghost of Hitler now roams through the popular mind in all the shapes that artifice and forgetfulness have combined to give him.

He will not go away soon. As fact, the "Thousand Year Reich" lasted little more than a decade, but as fiction it goes on and on. In the words of Horst Krüger, whose memoir of growing up in Nazi Germany is as prescient as any we have, this Hitler "has played a trick on us," "this Hitler remains with us—all the days of our lives."

# Discussion Questions

1. Henry Grosshans examines young Hitler's attempts to become an artist in Vienna. In the author's opinion, why did Hitler grow to detest Vienna? How did his hostility toward Vienna and his anti-Semitism contribute to his reaction to modern art?

2. Robert G.L. Waite presents evidence that Hitler was greatly influenced by two Viennese authors, Guido von List and Lanz von Liebenfels. What examples does Waite provide as proof that Hitler was familiar with the writings of these two men? In your opinion, does Waite provide sufficient proof? Why or why not?

3. Germany's crippling defeat in the First World War significantly affected Hitler, in Edleff H. Schwaab's view. What aspects of Germany's surrender confirmed Hitler's suspicions about an international Jewish conspiracy, according to Schwaab? What type of government did Hitler believe would restore Germany to its former glory?

4. The authors in this chapter provide a variety of factors that influenced Hitler in his early years. In your opinion, which of these, if any, was the most important in determining Hitler's later career? How might these different factors have interacted with each other in affecting Hitler? Cite examples from the articles to support your reasoning.

## Chapter Two

1. In the beginning of his essay, Joseph Nyomarkay describes the qualities and attributes of a charismatic leader. He then argues that Hitler was such a leader. What examples does Nyomarkay use to prove that Hitler fulfills the definition of a charismatic leader? Does the author give sufficient examples to make a successful argument, in your opinion? Defend your answer.

2. William Carr asserts that Hitler was one of the greatest orators of history. What arguments does Carr provide to

support this assertion? Do you find his reasoning convincing? Explain, citing examples from the text.

3. The economic and political atmosphere of postwar Germany made it possible for Hitler to come to power, contends Horst von Maltitz. According to the author, why did the majority of the German people despise the Weimar Republic? How did Hitler exploit this dissatisfaction in his play for power?

4. Robert G.L. Waite examines the intense popularity that Hitler garnered among young Germans. In Waite's opinion, for what specific reasons were young Germans drawn to Hitler? What aspects of Hitler's message especially appealed to this generation, and why?

5. Eberhard Jäckel argues that Hitler purposefully deceived the German people concerning his true nature and intentions. What evidence does Jäckel provide to support his contention? Do you find this evidence persuasive? Explain your answer.

**CHAPTER THREE**

1. In his essay, H.R. Trevor-Roper maintains that Hitler had established his aims for World War II early in his career and even published them in *Mein Kampf.* What three other documents does Trevor-Roper quote from to support his argument? Which of these four documents do you believe most supports his thesis, and why? In your opinion, does he provide sufficient evidence to support his claim? The author also admits that Hitler sometimes appeared to be modifying these plans or even taking advantage of opportunities as they arose. How does Trevor-Roper explain this in light of his theory concerning the consistency of Hitler's war aims? Are you convinced by his reasoning? Why or why not?

2. James V. Compton asserts that one of Hitler's primary mistakes in World War II was underestimating the threat presented by the United States. Sebastian Haffner maintains that Hitler's obsession with the Holocaust undermined his ability to win the war. What shortcomings in Hitler's military expertise do these two authors describe? What similarities do they note in Hitler's attitude toward the war?

3. Lucy S. Dawidowicz contends that Hitler planned the Holocaust early in his career but used coded language to disguise his intentions from those who might object. What examples does Dawidowicz give of this coded language? What evidence does William Carr provide to sup-

port his argument that Hitler did not have the Holocaust in mind until late in his career? In your opinion, which author presents the stronger case? Why?

## CHAPTER FOUR

1. Ian Kershaw and Norman Rich describe the impact Hitler had on Germany and the world. According to these authors, how does Hitler's final legacy differ from his plans and aims? How many negative effects of Hitler's legacy do these authors relate? How many positive effects, if any?

2. Since Hitler's death, popular culture has appropriated his image, writes Alvin H. Rosenfeld. Do you agree with Rosenfeld that novels, movies, and other works that deal with fictionalized versions of Hitler can be dangerous? Why or why not?

# APPENDIX

## EXCERPTS FROM ORIGINAL DOCUMENTS PERTAINING TO ADOLF HITLER

### DOCUMENT 1: CHILDHOOD TRAUMAS

*Written between 1924 and 1926, Adolf Hitler's book* Mein Kampf *("My Struggle") is part autobiography, part political manifesto. The following passage from* Mein Kampf *describes a young boy who witnesses his inebriated father violently attacking his mother. Several prominent historians and psychoanalysts have theorized that this passage actually reflects Hitler's own childhood experiences.*

Imagine, for instance, the following scene:

In a basement apartment, consisting of two stuffy rooms, dwells a worker's family of seven. Among the five children there is a boy of, let us assume, three years. This is the age in which the first impressions are made on the consciousness of the child. Talented persons retain traces of memory from this period down to advanced old age. The very narrowness and overcrowding of the room does not lead to favorable conditions. Quarreling and wrangling will very frequently arise as a result. In these circumstances, people do not live with one another, they press against one another. Every argument, even the most trifling, which in a spacious apartment can be reconciled by a mild segregation, thus solving itself, here leads to loathsome wrangling without end. Among the children, of course, this is still bearable; they always fight under such circumstances, and among themselves they quickly and thoroughly forget about it. But if this battle is carried on between the parents themselves, and almost every day in forms which for vulgarity often leave nothing to be desired, then, if only very gradually, the results of such visual instruction must ultimately become apparent in the children. The character they will inevitably assume if this mutual quarrel takes the form of brutal attacks of the father against the mother, of drunken beatings, is hard for anyone who does not know this milieu to imagine. At the age of six the pitiable little boy suspects the existence of things which can inspire even an adult with nothing but horror.

Adolf Hitler, *Mein Kampf,* trans. Ralph Manheim. Boston: Houghton Mifflin, 1943.

## DOCUMENT 2: HITLER'S CONFLICT WITH HIS FATHER

*Hitler's father had worked his way up from poverty to become a high-ranking customs official. He intended for his son to follow his footsteps in choosing a career. However, Hitler detested the thought of office work and wanted to become an artist. In the following excerpt from* Mein Kampf, *Hitler recounts the escalating battle between him and his father, as well as his decision to let his schoolwork deteriorate.*

It was decided that I should go to high school. . . .

It was [my father's] basic opinion and intention that, like himself, his son would and must become a civil servant. It was only natural that the hardships of his youth should enhance his subsequent achievement in his eyes, particularly since it resulted exclusively from his own energy and iron diligence. It was the pride of the self-made man which made him want his son to rise to the same position in life, or, of course, even higher if possible, especially since, by his own industrious life, he thought he would be able to facilitate his child's development so greatly.

It was simply inconceivable to him that I might reject what had become the content of his whole life. Consequently, my father's decision was simple, definite, and clear; in his own eyes I mean, of course. Finally, a whole lifetime spent in the bitter struggle for existence had given him a domineering nature, and it would have seemed intolerable to him to leave the final decision in such matters to an inexperienced boy, having as yet no sense of responsibility. Moreover, this would have seemed a sinful and reprehensible weakness in the exercise of his proper parental authority and responsibility for the future life of his child, and, as such, absolutely incompatible with his concept of duty.

And yet things were to turn out differently.

Then barely eleven years old, I was forced into opposition for the first time in my life. Hard and determined as my father might be in putting through plans and purposes once conceived, his son was just as persistent and recalcitrant in rejecting an idea which appealed to him not at all, or in any case very little.

I did not want to become a civil servant.

Neither persuasion nor 'serious' arguments made any impression on my resistance. I did not want to be a civil servant, no, and again no. All attempts on my father's part to inspire me with love or pleasure in this profession by stories from his own life accomplished the exact opposite. . . .

As long as my father's intention of making me a civil servant encountered only my theoretical distaste for the profession, the conflict was bearable. Thus far, I had to some extent been able to keep my private opinions to myself; I did not always have to contradict him immediately. My own firm determination never to become a civil servant sufficed to give me complete inner peace. And this decision in me was immutable. The problem became more difficult when I developed a plan of my own in opposition to my father's. And this occurred at the early age of twelve. How it happened, I myself do not know, but one day it became clear to me that I would become a painter, an artist. . . . When for the first time, after once again rejecting my father's favorite notion, I was asked what I myself wanted to be, and I rather abruptly blurted out the decision I had meanwhile made, my father for the moment was struck speechless.

'Painter? Artist?'

He doubted my sanity, or perhaps he thought he had heard wrong or misunderstood me. But when he was clear on the subject, and particularly after he felt the seriousness of my intention, he opposed it with all the determination of his nature. His decision was extremely simple, for any consideration of what abilities I might really have was simply out of the question.

'Artist, no, never as long as I live!' But since his son, among various other qualities, had apparently inherited his father's stubbornness, the same answer came back at him. Except, of course, that it was in the opposite sense.

And thus the situation remained on both sides. My father did not depart from his 'Never!' And I intensified my 'Oh, yes!'

The consequences, indeed, were none too pleasant. The old man grew embittered, and, much as I loved him, so did I. My father forbade me to nourish the slightest hope of ever being allowed to study art. I went one step further and declared that if that was the case I would stop studying altogether. As a result of such 'pronouncements,' of course, I drew the short end; the old man began the relentless enforcement of his authority. In the future, therefore, I was silent, but transformed my threat into reality.

Adolf Hitler, *Mein Kampf*, trans. Ralph Manheim. Boston: Houghton Mifflin, 1943.

## Document 3: Hitler's Early Encounters with Jews

*In this excerpt from* Mein Kampf, *Hitler writes that he had little contact with Jews or anti-Semitic thought until he moved to Vienna, where he was first exposed to Orthodox Jews dressed in their traditional costumes. This experience, he states, raised many questions in his mind, which he attempted to answer by reading anti-Semitic literature.*

Today it is difficult, if not impossible, for me to say when the word 'Jew' first gave me ground for special thoughts. At home I do not remember having heard the word during my father's lifetime. I believe that the old gentleman would have regarded any special emphasis on this term as cultural backwardness. In the course of his life he had arrived at more or less cosmopolitan views which, despite his pronounced national sentiments, not only remained intact, but also affected me to some extent. . . .

Not until my fourteenth or fifteenth year did I begin to come across the word 'Jew,' with any frequency, partly in connection with political discussions. This filled me with a mild distaste, and I could not rid myself of an unpleasant feeling that always came over me whenever religious quarrels occurred in my presence.

At that time I did not think anything else of the question.

There were few Jews in Linz. In the course of the centuries their outward appearance had become Europeanized and had taken on a human look; in fact, I even took them for Germans. The absurdity of this idea did not dawn on me because I saw no distinguishing feature but the strange religion. The fact that they had, as I believed, been persecuted on this account sometimes almost turned my distaste at unfavorable remarks about them into horror.

Thus far I did not so much as suspect the existence of an organized opposition to the Jews.

Then I came to Vienna. . . .

Once, as I was strolling through the Inner City, I suddenly encountered an apparition in a black caftan and black hair locks. Is this a Jew? was my first thought.

For, to be sure, they had not looked like that in Linz. I observed the man furtively and cautiously, but the longer I stared at this foreign face, scrutinizing feature for feature, the more my first question assumed a new form:

Is this a German?

As always in such cases, I now began to try to relieve my doubts by books. For a few hellers I bought the first anti-Semitic pamphlets of my life. . . .

I could no longer very well doubt that the objects of my study were not Germans of a special religion, but a people in themselves; for since I had begun to concern myself with this question and to take cognizance of the Jews, Vienna appeared to me in a different light than before. Wherever I went, I began to see Jews, and the more I saw, the more sharply they became distinguished in my eyes from the rest of humanity. Particularly the Inner City and the districts north of the Danube Canal swarmed with a people which even outwardly had lost all resemblance to Germans. . . .

The cleanliness of this people, moral and otherwise, I must say, is a point in itself. By their very exterior you could tell that these were no lovers of water, and, to your distress, you often knew it with your eyes closed. Later I often grew sick to my stomach from the smell of these caftan-wearers. Added to this, there was their unclean dress and their generally unheroic appearance.

All this could scarcely be called very attractive; but it became positively repulsive when, in addition to their physical uncleanliness, you discovered the moral stains on this 'chosen people.'

Adolf Hitler, *Mein Kampf,* trans. Ralph Manheim. Boston: Houghton Mifflin, 1943.

## DOCUMENT 4: THE END OF THE FIRST WORLD WAR

*In 1918, Hitler was caught in a British gas attack and temporarily blinded. While recuperating in a military hospital, he heard the news of the German surrender. In this passage from* Mein Kampf, *Hitler relates the emotional blow of the news—and his fateful decision that followed.*

In the night of October 13, the English gas attack on the southern front before Ypres burst loose; they used yellow-cross gas, whose effects were still unknown to us as far as personal experience was concerned. In this same night I myself was to become acquainted with it. On a hill south of Wervick, we came on the evening of October 13 into several hours of drumfire with gas shells which continued all night more or less violently. As early as midnight, a number of us passed out, a few of our comrades forever. Toward morning I, too, was seized with pain which grew worse with every quarter hour, and at seven in the morning I stumbled and tottered back with burning eyes; taking with me my last report of the War.

A few hours later, my eyes had turned into glowing coals; it had grown dark around me.

Thus I came to the hospital at Pasewalk in Pomerania, and there I was fated to experience—the greatest villainy of the century.

For a long time there had been something indefinite but repulsive in the air. People were telling each other that in the next few weeks it would 'start in'—but I was unable to imagine what was meant by this. . . . Even in the hospital, people were discussing the end of the War which they hoped would come soon, but no one counted on anything immediate. I was unable to read the papers.

In November the general tension increased. . . .

In the last few days I had been getting along better. The piercing pain in my eye sockets was diminishing; slowly I succeeded in distinguishing the broad outlines of the things about me. I was given grounds for hoping that I should recover my eyesight at least well enough to be able to pursue some profession later. To be sure, I could no longer hope that I would ever be able to draw again. In any case, I was on the road to improvement when the monstrous thing happened. . . .

On November 10, the pastor came to the hospital for a short address: now we learned everything.

In extreme agitation, I, too, was present at the short speech. The dignified old gentleman seemed all a-tremble as he informed us that the House of Hollenzollern should no longer bear the German imperial crown; that the fatherland had become a 'republic'; that we must pray to the Almighty not to refuse His blessing to this change and not to abandon our people in the times to come. He could not help himself, he had to speak a few words in memory of the royal house. He began to praise its services in Pomerania, in Prussia, nay, to the German fatherland, and—here he began to sob gently to himself—in the little hall the deepest dejection settled on all hearts, and I believe that not an eye was able to restrain its tears. But when the old gentleman tried to go on, and began to tell us that we must now end the long War, yes, that now that it was lost and we were throwing ourselves upon the mercy of the victors, our fatherland would for the future be exposed to dire oppression, that the armistice should be accepted with confidence in the magnanimity of our previous enemies—I could stand it no longer. It became impossible for me to sit still one minute more. Again everything went black before my eyes; I tottered and groped my way back to the dormitory, threw myself on my bunk, and dug my burning head into my blanket and pillow. . . .

Was it for this that the German soldier had stood fast in the sun's heat and in snowstorms, hungry, thirsty, and freezing, weary from sleepless nights and endless marches? Was it for this that he had lain in the hell of the drumfire and in the fever of gas attacks without wavering, always thoughtful of his one duty to preserve the fatherland from the enemy peril? . . .

The more I tried to achieve clarity on the monstrous event in this hour, the more the shame of indignation and disgrace burned my brow. What was all the pain in my eyes compared to this misery?

There followed terrible days and even worse nights—I knew that all was lost. Only fools, liars, and criminals could hope in the mercy of the enemy. In these nights hatred grew in me, hatred for those responsible for this deed. . . .

Kaiser William II was the first German Emperor to hold out a conciliatory hand to the leaders of Marxism, without suspecting that scoundrels have no honor. While they still held the imperial hand in theirs, their other hand was reaching for the dagger.

There is no making pacts with Jews; there can only be the hard: either—or.

I, for my part, decided to go into politics.

Adolf Hitler, *Mein Kampf,* trans. Ralph Manheim. Boston: Houghton Mifflin, 1943.

## DOCUMENT 5: THE NAZIS' FIRST MASS MEETING

*On February 24, 1920, the Nazi Party held its first large meeting in Munich, Germany. Hitler was the second speaker and presented the twenty-five points of the party's platform to the crowd. In the following excerpt from* Mein Kampf, *Hitler provides an account of the events of that night.*

The meeting was to be opened at 7:30. At 7:15 I entered the Festsaal of the Hofbräuhaus on the Platzl in Munich, and my heart nearly burst for joy. The gigantic hall—for at that time it still seemed to me gigantic—was overcrowded with people, shoulder to shoulder, a mass numbering almost two thousand people. And above all—those people to whom we wanted to appeal had come. Far more than half the hall seemed to be occupied by Communists and Independents [socialists]. They had resolved that our first demonstration would come to a speedy end.

But it turned out differently. After the first speaker had finished,

I took the floor. A few minutes later there was a hail of shouts, there were violent clashes in the hall, a handful of the most faithful war comrades and other supporters battled with the disturbers, and only little by little were able to restore order. I was able to go on speaking. After half an hour the applause slowly began to drown out the screaming and shouting.

I now took up the [National Socialist] program and began to explain it for the first time.

From minute to minute the interruptions were increasingly drowned out by shouts of applause. And when I finally submitted the twenty-five theses, point for point, to the masses and asked them personally to pronounce judgment on them, one after another was accepted with steadily mounting joy, unanimously and again unanimously, and when the last thesis had found its way to the heart of the masses, there stood before me a hall full of people united by a new conviction, a new faith, a new will.

When after nearly four hours the hall began to empty and the crowd, shoulder to shoulder, began to move, shove, press toward the exit like a slow stream, I knew that now the principles of a movement which could no longer be forgotten were moving out among the German people.

Adolf Hitler, *Mein Kampf,* trans. Ralph Manheim. Boston: Houghton Mifflin, 1943.

### DOCUMENT 6: HITLER ACCUSES THE JEWS OF EXPLOITING THE GERMANS

*From the beginning of his political career, Hitler employed his anti-Semitic beliefs in his speeches and writings. In this speech given in Munich on April 12, 1922, he depicts Jews—especially those who recently immigrated to Germany from Poland—as getting rich off of the labor of German workers. Contrasting the "fat" Jews against the thin and "ragged" Germans, Hitler vows to champion the German people in a fight for justice.*

I ask you: Did the Jews have an interest in the collapse of 1918? It is possible for us to discuss that objectively today. You are undoubtedly aware that on a comparative basis very few Jews have suffered at all. . . .

Look at those millions of workers in Berlin in 1914 and look at them today. Now they are thinner; their clothes ragged and torn; they are poverty-stricken.

And now take a look at the 100,000 Jews from the East who came here during the first years of the war. Most of them have gotten rich and even own automobiles. That is so not because the Jews are more clever, because I challenge you to say that millions of decent and hard-working citizens are only stupid people.

The only reason is that these 100,000 Jews were never really ready to work in an honorable manner in a national organism for the common good of all. From the beginning they regarded the whole national organism as nothing more than a hothouse in which they could thrive.

The Jew has not become poorer. Slowly he is puffing himself up. If you do not believe me, take a look at our health resorts. There you find two kinds of people: the German who tries to catch a breath of fresh air for the first time in a long while and who wants to recuperate; and the Jew, who goes to the resorts as a means of getting rid of his excess fat. When you go to the mountain resorts, whom do you find in new yellow shoes, with large knapsacks, in which you do not find much of anything? And why should they? The Jews travel to the hotel, usually as far as the train goes, and where the train stops, they also stop. They just sit within a kilometer of the hotel, like flies on a corpse.

Certainly this is not our own "working class," neither of our intellectual or laboring workers. You will usually find the "working classes" wearing old clothing, climbing about somewhere along the sides of the hotel, because they are ashamed to enter this perfumed atmosphere in their old clothes dating from 1913 and 1914. . . .

The Aryan looks upon work as the foundation of the national community. The Jew looks upon work as a means of exploiting others. The Jew never works as a productive creator but rather always with the idea of becoming a master. He works unproductively, utilizing and profiting from the work of others. . . .

I say this: My feeling as a Christian leads me to be a fighter for my Lord and Saviour. It leads me to the man who, at one time lonely and with only a few followers, recognized the Jews for what they were, and called on men to fight against them, and Who, believe me, was greatest not as a sufferer but as a fighter.

As a Christian and as a man with boundless love, I read that passage which told how the Lord finally gathered His strength and used the whip in order to drive the money-changers, the vipers, and the cheats from the temple. . . .

As a Christian, I owe something to my own people. I see how our people are working and working, laboring and exerting themselves, and still at the end of the week they have nothing but misery and poverty to show for it. That just is not understood in the homes of the nobility.

But when I go out in the mornings and see those people in the bread lines and look into their drawn faces, then I am convinced that I am really a devil and not a Christian if I do not feel compassion and do not wage war, as Christ did two thousand years ago, against those who are stealing from and exploiting these poverty-stricken people.

From Louis L. Snyder, ed., *Hitler's Third Reich: A Documentary History.* Chicago: Nelson-Hall, 1981.

## DOCUMENT 7: ALMOST A RELIGIOUS CONVERSION

*Kurt Ludecke joined the Nazi Party in its early days and spent much of his time working to spread the Nazi doctrine in the United States. During a visit to Berlin in 1933, Ludecke fell out of favor with Hitler and was imprisoned. He made a daring escape in February 1934, just a few months before Hitler's "Blood Purge" of the Nazi Party. Ludecke settled in America and published an account of his days as a Nazi, including this description of the August 11, 1922, demonstration in Munich at which he first saw Hitler.*

We were near the speakers' stand. I was close enough to see Hitler's face, watch every change in his expression, hear every word he said.

When the man stepped forward on the platform, there was almost no applause. He stood silent for a moment. Then he began to speak, quietly and ingratiatingly at first. Before long his voice had risen to a hoarse shriek that gave an extraordinary effect of an intensity of feeling. . . .

Critically I studied this slight, pale man, his brown hair parted on one side and falling again and again over his sweating brow. Threatening and beseeching, with small, pleading hands and flaming, steel-blue eyes, he had the look of a fanatic.

Presently my critical faculty was swept away. Leaning from the tribune as if he were trying to impel his inner self into the consciousness of all these thousands, he was holding the masses, and me with them, under a hypnotic spell by the sheer force of his conviction. . . .

I do not know how to describe the emotions that swept over me as I heard this man. His words were like a scourge. When he spoke of the disgrace of Germany, I felt ready to spring on any enemy. His appeal to German manhood was like a call to arms, the gospel he preached a sacred truth. He seemed another [Martin] Luther. I forgot everything but the man; then, glancing round, I saw that his magnetism was holding these thousands as one.

Of course I was ripe for this experience. I was a man of thirty-two, weary of disgust and disillusionment, a wanderer seeking a cause; a patriot without a channel for his patriotism, a yearner after the heroic without a hero. The intense will of the man, the passion of his sincerity seemed to flow from him into me. I experienced an exaltation that could be likened only to religious conversion.

I felt sure that no one who had heard Hitler that afternoon could doubt that he was the man of destiny, the vitalizing force in the future of Germany. . . .

I knew my search was ended. I had found myself, my leader, and my cause.

Kurt G.W. Ludecke, *I Knew Hitler: The Story of a Nazi Who Escaped the Blood Purge.* New York: Scribner's, 1937.

## DOCUMENT 8: HITLER'S CLOSING ARGUMENT AT HIS TREASON TRIAL

*In 1924, Hitler went on trial for organizing the November 1923 Beer Hall Putsch. Acting as his own lawyer, he admitted to planning to overthrow the Weimar Republic but vigorously defended his reasons for doing so. In this excerpt from his final speech to the court, Hitler maintains that the Nazi Party is becoming a powerful force that will redeem Germany's honor and pride.*

The army that we are building grows from day to day, from hour to hour. Right at this moment I have the proud hope that once the hour strikes these wild troops will merge into battalions, battalions into regiments, regiments into divisions. I have hopes that the old cockade will be lifted from the dirt, that the old colors will be unfurled to flutter again, that expiation will come before the tribunal of God. Then from our bones and from our graves will speak the voice of the only tribunal which has the right to sit in justice over us.

Then, gentlemen, not you will be the ones to deliver the verdict over us, but that verdict will be given by the eternal judgment of history, which will speak out against the accusation that has been made against us. I know what your judgment will be. But that other court will not ask us: Have you committed high treason or not? That court will judge us, the quartermaster-general of the old army, its officers and soldiers, who as Germans wanted only the best for their people and Fatherland, who fought and who were willing to die. You might just as well find us guilty a thousand times, but the goddess of the eternal court of history will smile and tear up the motions of the state's attorney and the judgment of this court: for she finds us not guilty.

From Louis L. Snyder, ed., *Hitler's Third Reich: A Documentary History.* Chicago: Nelson-Hall, 1981.

## DOCUMENT 9: LIVING SPACE FOR GERMANS

*Hitler began writing* Mein Kampf *during his prison stay in 1924. While some of the book was autobiographical, much of it set forth Hitler's political theories. In the following passage, he argues that Germany requires additional land in order to support its growing populace and suggests that this land should be taken from other countries by force. After Hitler gained control of Germany, obtaining "Lebensraum" (living space) was one of his primary goals.*

Germany has an annual increase in population of nearly nine hundred thousand souls. The difficulty of feeding this army of new citizens must grow greater from year to year and ultimately end in catastrophe, unless ways and means are found to forestall the danger of starvation and misery in time. . . .

As matters stand there are at the present time on this earth immense areas of unused soil, only waiting for the men to till them.

But it is equally true that Nature as such has not reserved this soil for the future possession of any particular nation or race; on the contrary, this soil exists for the people which possesses the force to take it and the industry to cultivate it. . . .

We must, therefore, coolly and objectively adopt the standpoint that it can certainly not be the intention of Heaven to give one people fifty times as much land and soil in this world as another. In this case we must not let political boundaries obscure for us the boundaries of eternal justice. If this earth really has room for all to live in, let us be given the soil we need for our livelihood.

True, they will not willingly do this. But then the law of self-preservation goes into effect; and what is refused to amicable methods, it is up to the fist to take. If our forefathers had let their decisions depend on the same pacifistic nonsense as our contemporaries, we should possess only a third of our present territory; but in that case there would scarcely be any German people for us to worry about in Europe today. . . .

For Germany . . . the only possibility for carrying out a healthy territorial policy [lies] in the acquisition of new land in Europe itself.

Adolf Hitler, *Mein Kampf,* trans. Ralph Manheim. Boston: Houghton Mifflin, 1943.

### Document 10: Responsibility, Command, and Obedience

*On January 27, 1932, Hitler delivered a speech to an important group of industrialists in Düsseldorf, Germany. Knowing that his audience was highly skeptical of him and his ideas, Hitler spent two and a half hours presenting the Nazi platform in rational, modulated tones. He won over his audience, and many of the attendees made substantial monetary contributions to the Nazi Party. In the following excerpt from this speech, Hitler describes the Nazi Party as a bulwark against Marxist communism.*

If anyone wants to accuse me as a National Socialist of the greatest possible crime, he says: "You want to force a decision by violence. You want one day to destroy your political opposition. We stand on the Constitution and the right of all political parties to exist." To that I reply: It is no good appealing for national unity when 50 percent of the people are pacifist and do not want to fight for the national colors. Any state which declares treason to the country to be ethical and moral does not deserve to live.

Gentlemen: Germany in the long run cannot exist unless we find our way back to a quite extraordinary, newly created political force which can exercise effective influence abroad. . . .

Today that movement cannot be destroyed. It is there. People must reckon with it whether they like it or not. They see before them an organization which does not preach as mere theory the views which today I have presented to you as essential, but puts them into practice. That organization is inspired to the highest degree by national sentiment, based on the idea of an absolute authority in leadership in all spheres. It has overcome not only internationalism but also democracy. It acknowledges only responsibility, command, and obedience. It has an indomitable aggressive spirit. It does not retire from the scene in cowardly fashion, but rather it brutally enforces its will and hurls to its enemies the retort: "We fight again! We fight tomorrow." It is no provocation when *German* Germany expresses itself.

We have formed an inexorable decision to destroy Marxism in Germany down to its last root. That decision does not come from love of brawling. I could easily have imagined a better life than one which means to be hunted throughout Germany, persecuted by countless government regulations, and with one foot in jail.

I could imagine for myself a better destiny than what was regarded by all as an insane chimera. I have been guided by nothing but my own faith, my indestructible confidence in the natural forces of our people, and by the necessity for good leadership.

From Louis L. Snyder, ed., *Hitler's Third Reich: A Documentary History.* Chicago: Nelson-Hall, 1981.

## DOCUMENT 11: HITLER'S ASCENT TO POWER

*Hitler was appointed as chancellor of Germany on January 30, 1933. That same day, he issued the following proclamation to the members of the Nazi Party.*

National Socialists! My Party Comrades!

A fourteen-year-long struggle, unparalleled in German history, has now culminated in a great political triumph.

The Reich President von Hindenburg has appointed me, the Führer of the National Socialist Movement, as Chancellor of the German Reich.

National leagues and parties have united in a joint fight for the resurrection of Germany.

The honor witnessed by German history of now being able to take a leading part in fulfilling this task I owe, next to the generous resolve of the Field Marshal, to your loyalty and devotion, my party comrades.

You followed me on cloudy days as unerringly as in the days of good fortune and remained true even after the most crushing defeats, and it is to that fact alone we owe this success.

Enormous is the task which lies before us. We must accomplish it, and we shall accomplish it.

Of you, my party comrades, I have only one major request: give me your confidence and your devotion in this new and great struggle, just as in the past, then the Almighty as well will not deny us His blessings toward reestablishing a German Reich of honor, freedom and domestic peace.

From Max Domarus, ed., *Hitler: Speeches and Proclamations, 1932–1945*, vol. 1, trans. Mary Fran Gilbert. Wauconda, IL: Bolchazy-Carducci, 1990.

### DOCUMENT 12: "THE GEORGE WASHINGTON OF GERMANY"

*Just as not all Germans supported Hitler, not all foreigners disap-
proved of him or his Nazi regime, especially prior to the war. Hitler
convinced many visitors that Germany had vastly improved under
his leadership and that he only wanted peace. In the following selection, David Lloyd George, a member of the British Parliament
and a former prime minister, gives his impressions of Nazi Germany
after a three-week visit in the fall of 1936.*

I have just returned from a visit to Germany. In so short a time one
can only form impressions or at least check impressions which
years of distant observation through the telescope of the Press and
constant inquiry from those who have seen things at a closer range
had already made on one's mind.

I have now seen the famous German Leader and also something
of the great change he has effected.

Whatever one may think of his methods—and they are certainly
not those of a parliamentary country—there can be no doubt that
he has achieved a marvellous transformation in the spirit of the
people, in their attitude towards each other, and in their social and
economic outlook. . . .

One man has accomplished this miracle. He is a born leader of
men. A magnetic, dynamic personality with a single-minded purpose, a resolute will and a dauntless heart.

He is not merely in name but in fact the national Leader. He has
made them safe against potential enemies by whom they were surrounded. He is also securing them against that constant dread of
starvation which is one of the poignant memories of the last years
of the War and the first years of the Peace. Over 700,000 died of
sheer hunger in those dark years. You can still see the effect in the
physique of those who were born into that bleak world.

The fact that Hitler has rescued his country from the fear of a
repetition of that period of despair, penury and humiliation has
given him unchallenged authority in modern Germany.

As to his popularity, especially among the youth of Germany,
there can be no manner of doubt. The old trust him; the young
idolise him. It is not the admiration accorded to a popular Leader.
It is the worship of a national hero who has saved his country from
utter despondency and degradation.

It is true that public criticism of the Government is forbidden in
every form. That does not mean that criticism is absent. I have
heard the speeches of prominent Nazi orators freely condemned.

But not a word of criticism or of disapproval have I heard of
Hitler.

He is as immune from criticism as a king in a monarchical
country. He is something more. He is the George Washington of
Germany—the man who won for his country independence from
all her oppressors.

To those who have not actually seen and sensed the way Hitler reigns over the heart and mind of Germany this description may appear extravagant. All the same, it is the bare truth. This great people will work better, sacrifice more, and, if necessary, fight with greater resolution because Hitler asks them to do so. Those who do not comprehend this central fact cannot judge the present possibilities of modern Germany.

David Lloyd George, "I Talked to Hitler," *Daily Express*, November 17, 1936.

## Document 13: Hitler's Response to President Roosevelt

*Alarmed by Hitler's territorial advances in Europe, President Franklin D. Roosevelt sent him a message on April 15, 1939, urging him to agree to a ten-year truce. On April 23, Hitler called a meeting of the German parliament and read the members his response. In this excerpt, Hitler assures Roosevelt that he does not intend to invade certain countries and then attempts to justify his actions in Austria and Czechoslovakia by drawing parallels between Germany and the United States.*

Members of the German *Reichstag*! The President of the United States of America has addressed a telegram to me with the curious contents of which you are already familiar. Before I, the addressee, actually received the document the rest of the world had already been informed of it by radio and newspaper reports. . . .

In view of these facts I decided to summon the German *Reichstag* so that you gentlemen might have the opportunity of hearing my answer first, and of either confirming that answer or rejecting it. In addition, I considered it desirable to keep to the method of procedure initiated by President Roosevelt and to inform the rest of the world on my part and by our means of my answer. . . .

Mr. Roosevelt asks that assurance be given him that the German armed forces will not attack, and above all, not invade, the territory or possessions of the following independent nations he then names as those coming into question: Finland, Latvia, Estonia, Norway, Sweden, Denmark, the Netherlands, Belgium, Great Britain, Ireland, France, Portugal, Spain, Switzerland, Liechtenstein, Luxemburg, Poland, Hungary, Turkey, Iraq, the Arabias, Syria, Palestine, Egypt, and Iran.

The answer: I have first taken the trouble to ascertain from the States mentioned, firstly, whether they feel themselves threatened, and secondly and above all, whether this inquiry by the American President was addressed to us at their suggestion, or at any rate, with their consent.

The reply was in all cases negative, in some instances strongly so. . . .

Mr. Roosevelt! I fully understand that the vastness of your nation and the immense wealth of your country allow you to feel responsible for the history of the whole world and for the history of all nations. I, sir, am placed in a much more modest and smaller sphere. You have 130,000,000 people on 9,500,000 square kilometers.

You possess a country with enormous riches in all mineral resources, fertile enough to feed a half-billion people and to provide them with all necessities.

I once took over a State which was faced by complete ruin, thanks to its trust in the promises of the rest of the world and to the bad regime of democratic governments. In this State there are roughly 140 people to each square kilometer—not 15, as in America. The fertility of our country cannot be compared with that of yours.

We lack numerous minerals which nature has placed at your disposal in unlimited quantities.

Billions of German savings accumulated in gold and foreign exchange during many years of peace were squeezed out of us and taken from us. We lost our colonies. In 1933 I had in my country 7,000,000 unemployed, a few million workers on half-time, millions of peasants sinking into poverty, destroyed trade, ruined commerce; in short, general chaos.

Since then, Mr. Roosevelt, I have only been able to fulfill one simple task. I cannot feel myself responsible for the fate of the world, as this world took no interest in the pitiful state of my own people. . . .

I have succeeded in finding useful work once more for the whole of 7,000,000 unemployed, who so appeal to the hearts of us all, in keeping the German peasant on his soil in spite of all difficulties, and in saving the land itself for him, in once more bringing German trade to a peak and in assisting traffic to the utmost.

As precaution against the threats of another world war, not only have I united the German people politically, but I have also rearmed them. . . .

I have brought back to the Reich provinces stolen from us in 1919; I have led back to their native country millions of Germans who were torn away from us and were in misery; I have reestablished the historic unity of German living space and, Mr. Roosevelt, I have endeavored to attain all this without spilling blood and without bringing to my people, and consequently to others, the misery of war.

From Louis L. Snyder, ed., *Hitler's Third Reich: A Documentary History.* Chicago: Nelson-Hall, 1981.

## DOCUMENT 14: THE DECLARATION OF WAR AGAINST POLAND

*World War II officially started on September 1, 1939, when Germany began to bomb Poland. On that day, Hitler put on a military uniform and vowed not to wear civilian clothes again until Germany won the war. He also delivered the following speech, in which he gave his version of the events leading up to Germany's military action against Poland.*

Deputies, Men of the German Reichstag!

For months a problem has tormented all of us. Long ago the Dik-tat [Treaty] of Versailles bestowed this problem on us. In its de-pravity and degeneracy it has now become insufferable. Danzig was a German city and is a German city! The Corridor was German and is German!

These regions owe their cultural development exclusively to the German Volk [people]. Without this Volk, these eastern regions would still be plunged in the depths of barbarism.

Danzig was torn from us! Poland annexed the Corridor! The German minorities living there are being persecuted in the vilest manner imaginable. In the years 1919 and 1920 over one million men of German blood were forced to leave their homeland.

As always, I sought to bring about a change by peaceful means, by offering proposals to remedy this situation which meanwhile had become unbearable. . . .

You know that all these proposals were rejected. . . .

And not only this! They were answered by mobilization, aug-mented terror, increasing pressure on ethnic Germans in these regions. . . .

Poland has unleashed this war against the Free City of Danzig! . . .

Last night I informed the British Government that, under the cir-cumstances, I no longer see any willingness by the Polish Govern-ment to enter into serious negotiations with us. And thus all at-tempts at mediation must be considered to have failed. For we had indeed received a response to our proposals which consisted of:

1. general mobilization in Poland and

2. renewed, heinous atrocities.

Similar events repeated themselves in the course of last night. And this after the recent perpetration of twenty-one border trans-gressions in the span of one single night. Yesterday fourteen addi-tional violations of the border were recorded, among them three of a most serious nature. I have therefore resolved to speak to Poland in the same language that Poland has employed towards us in the months past. . . .

I am . . . determined to wage this war until the present Polish Government judges it opportune to assent to these changes, or an-other Polish Government shall be willing to do so.

I will cleanse Germany's borders of this element of insecurity, this civil-war-like circumstance. I will take care that our border in the East enjoys the same peace as along any other of our bor-ders. . . .

This night for the first time Polish regular soldiers fired on our own territory. We have now been returning the fire since 5:45 a.m.! Henceforth, bomb will be met with bomb.

He who fights with poison shall be fought with poison gas. He

who distances himself from the rules for a humane conduct of warfare can only expect us to take like steps. I will lead this struggle,
whoever may be the adversary, until the security of the Reich and
its rights have been assured. . . .

I now wish to be nothing other than the first soldier of the German Reich. Therefore I have put on that [military] tunic which has
always been the most holy and dear to me. I shall not take it off
again until after victory is ours, or—I shall not live to see the day! . . .

Since I myself stand ever ready to lay down my life for my Volk
and Germany, I demand the same of everyone else! Whoever believes he can oppose this national commandment shall fall! We will
have nothing to do with traitors!

And all of us pledge ourselves to the one ancient principle: it is
of no importance if we ourselves live—as long as our Volk lives, as
long as Germany lives!

From Max Domarus, ed., *Hitler: Speeches and Proclamations, 1932–1945*, vol. 3, trans.
Chris Wilcox. Wauconda, IL: Bolchazy-Carducci, 1997.

### DOCUMENT 15: HITLER'S MENTAL STATE

*Hermann Rauschning was the mayor of Danzig (Gdansk), a city
that both Germany and Poland claimed. Rauschning originally allied with Hitler, but he later broke from the Nazis and became a
scathing critic of the Nazi regime. In the following excerpt from* The
Voice of Destruction, *Rauschning sheds light on Hitler's erratic be-
havior and unstable personality.*

Is Hitler mad?

I think everyone who has met the Führer two or three times
must have asked himself this question. Anyone who has seen this
man face to face, has met his uncertain glance, without depth or
warmth, from eyes that seem hard and remote, and has then seen
that gaze grow rigid, will certainly have experienced the uncanny
feeling: "That man is not normal."

Then again he may be seen to sit in apathy for a quarter of an
hour, without speaking a word, without even looking up, picking
his teeth abominably. Has he heard anything that was going on?
Has he been dreaming? Never was a real conversation with Hitler
possible. Either he would listen in silence, or he would "speechify"
and not allow one to speak. Or he would walk restlessly up and
down, interrupt constantly, and jump from one subject to another
as if unable to concentrate.

I cannot judge whether Hitler is near madness in the clinical
sense. My own experience of him and what I have learned from
others indicate a lack of control amounting to total demoralization.
His shrieking and frenzied shouting, his stamping, his tempests of
rage—all this was grotesque and unpleasant, but it was not madness. When a grown-up man lashes out against the walls like a
horse in its stall, or throws himself on the ground his conduct may

be morbid, but it is more certainly rude and undisciplined.

Hitler, however, has states that approach persecution mania and dual personality. His sleeplessness is more than the mere result of excessive nervous strain. He often wakes up in the middle of the night and wanders restlessly to and fro. Then he must have light everywhere. Lately he has sent at these times for young men who have to keep him company during his hours of manifest anguish. At times these conditions must have become dreadful. . . .

I have frequently heard men confess that they are afraid of him, that they, grown men though they are, cannot visit him without a beating heart. They have the feeling that the man will suddenly spring at them and strangle them, or throw the inkpot at them, or do something senseless. . . .

I have often had the opportunity of examining my own experience, and I must admit that in Hitler's company I have again and again come under a spell which I was only later able to shake off, a sort of hypnosis. He is, indeed, a remarkable man. It leads nowhere to depreciate him and speak mockingly of him. He is simply a sort of great medicine-man. He is literally that, in the full sense of the term. We have gone back so far toward the savage state that the medicine-man has become king among us.

Hermann Rauschning, *The Voice of Destruction.* New York: G.P. Putnam's Sons, 1940.

## DOCUMENT 16: HITLER'S REVENGE

*In June 1940, Germany's forces overran France. On June 21, Hitler met with French envoys to discuss terms for France's surrender. Hitler insisted that the meeting take place at the same spot where in 1918 German officials had signed the armistice that ended World War I. The following eyewitness account of the events of that day was written by William L. Shirer, a reporter for CBS radio.*

On the exact spot in the little clearing in the Forest of Compiègne where at five a.m. on November 11, 1918 the armistice which ended the World War was signed, Adolf Hitler today handed *his* armistice terms to France. To make German revenge complete, the meeting of the German and French plenipotentiaries took place in Marshal Foch's private car, in which Foch laid down the armistice terms to Germany twenty-two years ago. Even the same table in the rickety old *wagon-lit* car was used. And through the windows we saw Hitler occupying the very seat on which Foch had sat at that table when he dictated the other armistice.

The humiliation of France, of the French, was complete. And yet in the preamble to the armistice terms Hitler told the French that he had not chosen this spot at Compiègne out of revenge; merely to right an old wrong. From the demeanour of the French delegates I gathered that they did not appreciate the difference. . . .

The armistice negotiations began at three fifteen p.m. A warm June sun beat down on the great elm and pine trees, and cast pleasant shadows on the wooded avenues as Hitler, with the German plenipotentiaries at his side, appeared. . . .

I observed his face. It was grave, solemn, yet brimming with revenge. There was also in it, as in his springy step, a note of the triumphant conqueror, the defier of the world. There was something else, difficult to describe, in his expression, a sort of scornful, inner joy at being present at this great reversal of fate—a reversal he himself had wrought.

Now he reaches the little opening in the woods. He pauses and looks slowly around. . . .

Hitler's personal flag is run up on a small standard in the centre of the opening.

Also in the centre is a great granite block which stands some three feet above the ground. Hitler, followed by the others, walks slowly over to it, steps up, and reads the inscription engraved in great high letters on that block. It says: "HERE ON THE ELEVENTH OF NOVEMBER 1918 SUCCUMBED THE CRIMINAL PRIDE OF THE GERMAN EMPIRE . . . VANQUISHED BY THE FREE PEOPLES WHICH IT TRIED TO ENSLAVE."

Hitler reads it. . . . They all read it, standing there in the June sun and the silence. I look for the expression on Hitler's face. I am but fifty yards from him and see him through my glasses as though he were directly in front of me. I have seen that face many times at the great moments of his life. But today! It is afire with scorn, anger, hate, revenge, triumph. He steps off the monument and contrives to make even this gesture a masterpiece of contempt. He glances back at it, contemptuous, angry—angry, you almost feel, because he cannot wipe out the awful, provoking lettering with one sweep of his high Prussian boot. He glances slowly around the clearing, and now, as his eyes meet ours, you grasp the depth of his hatred. But there is triumph there too—revengeful, triumphant hate. Suddenly, as though his face were not giving quite complete expression to his feelings, he throws his whole body into harmony with his mood. He swiftly snaps his hands on his hips, arches his shoulders, plants his feet wide apart. It is a magnificent gesture of defiance, of burning contempt for this place now and all that it has stood for in the twenty-two years since it witnessed the humbling of the German Empire.

William L. Shirer, *Berlin Diary: The Journal of a Foreign Correspondent, 1934–1941.* New York: Alfred A. Knopf, 1943.

## DOCUMENT 17: NO OTHER SOLUTION THAN EXTERMINATION

*On an almost daily basis, usually during informal meals with his intimate circle of trusted Nazis, Hitler would expound on his theories in long monologues. Between 1941 and 1944, he allowed a secretary to take notes during these talks, which after his death were published as* Hitler's Table Talk. *In the following passage from January 23,*

*1942, Hitler reveals his intent to exterminate the Jews and places the blame for World War II on their shoulders.*

One must act radically. When one pulls out a tooth, one does it with a single tug, and the pain quickly goes away. The Jew must clear out of Europe. Otherwise no understanding will be possible between Europeans. It's the Jew who prevents everything. When I think about it, I realise that I'm extraordinarily humane. At the time of the rule of the Popes, the Jews were mistreated in Rome. Until 1830, eight Jews mounted on donkeys were led once a year through the streets of Rome. For my part, I restrict myself to telling them they must go away. If they break their pipes on the journey, I can't do anything about it. But if they refuse to go voluntarily, I see no other solution but extermination. Why should I look at a Jew through other eyes than if he were a Russian prisoner-of-war? In the p.o.w. camps, many are dying. It's not my fault. I didn't want either the war or the p.o.w. camps. Why did the Jew provoke this war?

*Hitler's Table Talk, 1941–44: His Private Conversations,* trans. Norman Cameron and R.H. Stevens. London: Weidenfeld and Nicolson, 1953.

## DOCUMENT 18: PLANS FOR THE UKRAINE AND RUSSIA

*In an after-dinner "table talk" on July 22, 1942, Hitler explains his intentions for Russia and the other eastern territories once they are conquered. The local inhabitants, whom he planned to use as slave labor, were to receive very little education and be strictly segregated from the German settlers in the area.*

The local population must be given no facilities for higher education. A failure on our part in this respect would simply plant the seeds of future opposition to our rule. Schools, of course, they must have—and they must pay for their tuition. But there is no need to teach them much more than, say, the meaning of the various road-signs. Instruction in geography can be restricted to one single sentence: The Capital of the Reich is Berlin, a city which everyone should try to visit once in his lifetime. Finally, elementary instruction in reading and writing in German will complete the course. Mathematics and such like are quite unnecessary.

In setting up the educational system, the same principles apply to both Eastern territories and any other colonies. We do not want any of this enlightenment nonsense propagated by an advance guard of parsons! What is the use of talking about progress to people like that? [General Alfred] Jodl is quite right when he says that notices in the Ukrainian language "Beware of the Trains" are superfluous; what on earth does it matter if one or two more locals get run over by the trains? . . .

Germans will in no circumstances live in a Ukrainian town. If essential, it will be better to put Germans in barracks outside a town than to allow them to live inside it. Otherwise, sooner or later, the process of cleaning up and improving the town will inevitably start;

and Russian and Ukrainian towns are not in any circumstances to be improved or made more habitable. It is not our mission to lead the local inhabitants to a higher standard of life; and our ultimate object must be to build towns and villages exclusively for Germans and absolutely separate from Russian or Ukrainian towns.

*Hitler's Table Talk, 1941–44: His Private Conversations*, trans. Norman Cameron and R.H. Stevens. London: Weidenfeld and Nicolson, 1953.

### DOCUMENT 19: AN ASSASSINATION ATTEMPT FAILS

*On July 20, 1944, Hitler survived an assassination attempt carried out by a group of German military officers. Immediately thereafter, he broadcast this message over the radio to reassure the German people that he was alive and well.*

German men and women: I do not know how many times an attempt on my life has been planned and carried out. If I address you today I am doing so for two reasons: first, so that you shall hear my voice and know that I personally am unhurt and well and, second, so that you shall hear the details about a crime that has no equal in German history.

An extremely small clique of ambitious, unscrupulous and at the same time foolish, criminally stupid, officers hatched a plot to remove me and, together with me, virtually to exterminate the staff of the German High Command. The bomb that was placed by Col. Graf von Stauffenberg exploded two meters [slightly more than two yards] away from me on my right side. It wounded very seriously a number of my dear collaborators. One of them has died. I personally am entirely unhurt apart from negligible grazes, bruises or burns.

This I consider to be confirmation of the task given to me by Providence to continue in pursuit of the aim of my life, as I have done hitherto. . . .

I am convinced that every decent officer and every brave soldier will understand at this hour what fate would have overtaken Germany if the attempt today had succeeded. Only very few, perhaps, are capable of visualizing the consequences. I myself thank providence and the Lord, not because I have been spared—my life is only care and work for my people—I thank them that I shall be allowed in the future also to carry this burden and to carry on with my work to the best of my abilities, as I have to answer for it with my conscience and before my conscience.

From Louis L. Snyder, ed., *Hitler's Third Reich: A Documentary History*. Chicago: Nelson-Hall, 1981.

### DOCUMENT 20: THE END NEARS

*Hitler spent his final days in an underground bunker in Berlin, surrounded by the most loyal of his associates and staff. Albert Speer, Hitler's personal architect, was among those who remained to the*

*bitter end. Speer later described Hitler's physical and mental deteri-
oration in his memoir entitled* Inside the Third Reich, *from which
the following passage is taken.*

In the last weeks of his life, Hitler seemed to have broken out of the
rigidity which had gradually overcome him during the preceding
years. He became more accessible again and could even tolerate
the expression of dissent. As late as the winter of 1944, it would
have been inconceivable for him to enter into a discussion of the
prospects of the war with me. Then, too, his flexibility on the question of the scorched earth policy would have been unthinkable, or
the quiet way he went over my radio speech. He was once more
open to arguments he would not have listened to a year ago. But
this greater softness sprang not from a relaxation of tension.
Rather, it was dissolution. He gave the impression of a man whose
whole purpose had been destroyed, who was continuing along his
established orbit only because of the kinetic energy stored within
him. Actually, he had let go of the controls and was resigned to
what might come. . . .

Now, he was shriveling up like an old man. His limbs trembled;
he walked stooped, with dragging footsteps. Even his voice became
quavering and lost its old masterfulness. Its force had given way to
a faltering, toneless manner of speaking. When he became excited,
as he frequently did in a senile way, his voice would start breaking.
He still had his fits of obstinacy, but they no longer reminded one
of a child's temper tantrums, but of an old man's. His complexion
was sallow, his face swollen; his uniform, which in the past he had
kept scrupulously neat, was often neglected in this last period of
life and stained by the food he had eaten with a shaking hand.

This condition undoubtedly touched his entourage, who had
been at his side during the triumphs of his life. I too was constantly
tempted to pity him, so reduced was he from the Hitler of the past.
Perhaps that was the reason everyone would listen to him in silence when, in the long since hopeless situation, he continued to
commit nonexistent divisions or to order units supplied by planes
that could no longer fly for lack of fuel. . . .

For some time Hitler had abandoned the upper rooms. He
claimed that the constant air raids disturbed his sleep and inter-
fered with his ability to work. In the bunker he could at least get
some sleep, he said. And so he had converted to an underground
life.

This withdrawal into his future tomb had, for me, a symbolic
significance as well. The isolation of this bunker world, encased on
all sides by concrete and earth, put the final seal on Hitler's separation from the tragedy which was going on outside under the open
sky. He no longer had any relationship to it. When he talked about
the end, he meant his own and not that of the nation. He had
reached the last station in his flight from reality, a reality which he

had refused to acknowledge since his youth. At the time I had a name for this unreal world of the bunker: I called it the Isle of the Departed.

Albert Speer, *Inside the Third Reich*, trans. Richard and Clara Winston. New York: Macmillan, 1970.

### DOCUMENT 21: HITLER'S LAST POLITICAL TESTAMENT

*On April 29, 1945, Hitler dictated his private will and his final testament, the latter of which is excerpted here. To the last, he expressed his vehement hatred of Jews, blaming them for the war and urging the German people to continue battling against "International Jewry." The following day, as Russian troops invaded Berlin, Hitler committed suicide in his underground bunker.*

More than thirty years have passed since I made my modest contribution in 1914 as a volunteer in the First World War, a war which was forced upon the Reich.

In these three decades, all my thoughts, all my deeds, and all other aspects of my life were motivated only by my love of my people and by my loyalty to them. They gave me the strength to make the most difficult decisions that have ever confronted mortal man. In these three decades I have exhausted my time, my working strength, and my health.

It is not true that I or anybody else in Germany, wanted war in 1939. It was wanted and provoked exclusively by those international statesmen who either were of Jewish origin or worked for Jewish interests. I have made too many offers for the restriction and control of armaments—which posterity will not be able to ignore forever—for responsibility for the outbreak of this war to be placed on me. Moreover, I have never wished that the first terrible world war should be followed by a second one against England, let alone America. Centuries will pass, but from the ruins of our towns and monuments hatred of those ultimately responsible will always grow anew, those whom we have to thank for all this: International Jewry and its helpers! . . .

After a six-year struggle, which in spite of all setbacks will one day go down in history as the most glorious and heroic manifestation of a people's will to live, I cannot forsake the city that is the capital of this Reich. Since our forces are too small to hold out any longer against the enemy's assault on this place, . . . I wish to share the fate that millions of others have accepted by staying here in this city. Besides, I do not wish to fall into the hands of an enemy who requires a new spectacle, staged by the Jews, to amuse his frenzied masses.

I have therefore decided to remain in Berlin and there to choose death voluntarily at the moment when I believe that the residence of the Führer and Chancellor can no longer be held. I die with a happy heart in view of my knowledge of the immeasurable deeds and accomplishments of our soldiers at the front, our women at home, the achievements of our farmers and workers, and the military efforts—unique in history—of our youth which bears my name.

That I express my thanks to all of you from the bottom of my heart is just as self-evident as my wish that you will therefore under no circumstances give up the struggle but will carry it on against the enemies of the Fatherland. . . .

Many of the most courageous men and women have decided to tie their lives to mine right to the end. I have begged and finally ordered them not to do this, but rather to take part in the nation's continuing struggle. . . .

Above all, I enjoin the leaders of the nation and those under them to uphold the racial laws to their full extent and to oppose mercilessly the universal poisoner of all peoples, International Jewry.

From George H. Stein, ed., *Hitler*. Englewood Cliffs, NJ: Prentice-Hall, 1968.

# CHRONOLOGY

**JANUARY 7, 1885**

Alois Hitler and Klara Pölzl marry. Between 1885 and 1887, Klara gives birth to two sons and a daughter.

**1887–1888**

The three children of Alois and Klara Hitler die within a few months of each other.

**APRIL 20, 1889**

Adolf Hitler is born in Braunau am Inn, Austria.

**1894**

Adolf's brother Edmund is born.

**1895**

Alois Hitler retires from the civil service.

**1896**

Adolf's sister Paula is born.

**1900**

Edmund dies from measles. Adolf begins classes at the Realschule (secondary school) in Linz, Austria.

**1903**

Alois Hitler dies suddenly.

**1905**

Adolf leaves school without earning a diploma.

**1907**

Klara Hitler is diagnosed with cancer early in the year. Adolf travels to the Austrian capital of Vienna to take the entrance examinations for the General Painting School of the Vienna Academy of Fine Arts, but he is refused admission. His mother dies in December.

**1908**

Adolf Hitler moves to Vienna, sharing lodgings with a friend. He again tries, without success, to gain entrance to the Academy of Fine Arts. In November, Hitler moves to new lodgings without informing his roommate or his family.

## 1909–1913

Hitler drifts into an aimless existence in Vienna, at one point residing in a homeless shelter. He primarily supports himself by selling small paintings. In mid-1913, he relocates to the city of Munich, in the southern German region of Bavaria.

## 1914

World War I begins; Hitler enlists with the Sixteenth Bavarian Reserve Infantry Regiment.

## 1918

Hitler is awarded the Iron Cross first class for bravery in August. In October, he is temporarily blinded by poison gas during a British attack. While recuperating in a military hospital, he learns that Germany has surrendered to the Allies. Discharged from the hospital in November, Hitler is transferred to the Second Bavarian Infantry Regiment in Munich.

## 1919

Serving as an informant for the German military, Hitler attends meetings of fringe political organizations. In June, Germany signs the Treaty of Versailles. On September 12, Hitler attends a meeting of a small political group called the German Workers' Party. He joins the party shortly thereafter and is quickly admitted into the inner circle of leaders.

## 1920

In February, the German Workers' Party changes its name to the National Socialist German Workers' Party, later abbreviated to the Nazi Party. The group also adopts the swastika as its official symbol. On February 24, Hitler presents the party's twenty-five-point program at a mass meeting in a Munich beer hall. He resigns from the German army on March 31 in order to devote all his time to politics, becoming the chief propaganda officer of the party.

## 1921

In July, Hitler threatens to resign from the Nazi Party unless he is made party chairman and given dictatorial powers. His demands are met, and he begins using the title Führer (leader).

## 1923

At a Munich beer hall on November 8, Hitler announces the beginning of a national revolution, or putsch. The Nazis march through Munich the next day, but their attempted coup comes to a sudden end when police open fire on the procession. Hitler goes into hiding but is captured on November 11 and is arrested for his role in instigating the Beer Hall Putsch. The Nazi Party is banned.

## 1924

Hitler stands trial for high treason and is sentenced to five years in prison. While serving time in Landsberg Prison, he writes the first volume of *Mein Kampf* ("My Struggle"). In December, Hitler is pardoned and released from Landsberg.

## 1925

Hitler revives the Nazi Party in February. The first volume of *Mein Kampf* is published in July. Hitler writes the second volume of *Mein Kampf*. His half-sister Angela Raubal moves in with him to be his housekeeper, bringing along her seventeen-year-old daughter, Geli.

## 1926

The second volume of *Mein Kampf* is published in December.

## 1928

During the national elections in May, the Nazi Party receives only 2.6 percent of the vote, obtaining twelve seats in the German Reichstag (parliament).

## 1929

Hitler is introduced to seventeen-year-old Eva Braun, who will become his longtime mistress. In October, the U.S. stock market crashes, initiating a worldwide economic depression.

## 1930

Germany begins to experience severe economic problems due to the Great Depression. In the Reichstag elections held in September, the Nazis win 107 seats, becoming Germany's second-strongest party.

## 1931

In September, Geli Raubal is found shot to death in Hitler's Munich apartment, an apparent suicide. Hitler is so distraught over her death that he comes close to suicide himself.

## 1932

Hitler becomes a German citizen in February. He runs for president but loses to the incumbent, Paul von Hindenburg. In the Reichstag elections, the Nazis win 230 seats and become the strongest party in the Reichstag.

## 1933

Hindenburg appoints Hitler chancellor of Germany on January 30. In the March elections, the Nazis gain 288 seats in the Reichstag. On March 23, the Reichstag passes the Enabling Act, effectively making Hitler dictator. All political parties except the Nazis are outlawed on July 14. In the November elections, the Nazis win 92.2 percent of the vote; they now completely dominate the Reichstag.

## 1934

On June 30, Hitler orders the arrest and execution of his enemies, including many within the Nazi Party; this event becomes known as the Blood Purge or the Night of the Long Knives. After Hindenburg's death on August 2, Hitler combines the offices of president and chancellor, declaring himself the Führer of Germany.

## 1935

The Saar district, which has been under the governorship of the League of Nations since World War I, overwhelmingly votes to be reincorporated into Germany. On March 16, Hitler reintroduces a general military draft in violation of the Treaty of Versailles. On September 15, the anti-Jewish Nuremberg Laws are passed.

## 1936

On March 7, Hitler sends German troops to occupy the demilitarized Rhineland. In September, he announces the Four-Year Plan, designed to prepare the German economy for a large-scale war. Germany and Japan sign the Anti-Comintern Pact on November 25.

## 1937

In September, Hitler and Italian dictator Benito Mussolini formalize their alliance, known as the Rome-Berlin Axis. Italy joins the Anti-Comintern Pact on November 6.

## 1938

German troops invade Austria on March 12; the next day, Hitler signs a law reunifying Germany and Austria. During the Munich Conference in September, the Allies attempt to appease Hitler by giving him the Sudetenland, a region of Czechoslovakia that is highly German in ethnicity. On November 9 and 10, the Nazis incite a violent rampage against German Jews that becomes known as Kristallnacht (Crystal Night, or the Night of the Broken Glass).

## 1939

In mid-March, the German army occupies the rest of Czechoslovakia. On August 23, Hitler and Soviet dictator Joseph Stalin sign a nonaggression pact that contains a secret clause determining the division of Poland. Germany invades Poland on September 1, starting World War II. Great Britain and France declare war on Germany on September 3.

## 1940

Hitler's troops invade Norway and Denmark on April 9. On May 10, Hitler attacks Belgium, Holland, and Luxembourg. The German army continues into France, which signs an armistice with Germany on June 21. In August, the German Luftwaffe (air force) begins to attack Great Britain but suffers heavy losses in the Battle of Britain. On September 27, Germany, Italy, and Japan sign the Tripartite Pact.

## 1941

Germany invades Yugoslavia and Greece on April 6. The German assault on the Soviet Union begins on June 22. In October, Hitler prematurely declares the Soviet Union defeated. The first Nazi death camp opens at Chelmno, Poland, in December. On December 7, Japan bombs Pearl Harbor. Hitler declares war on the United States on December 11.

## 1942

At the Wannsee Conference on January 20, the Nazi leaders draw up their plans for the Final Solution—the genocide of the Jewish people. In late March, the Nazis begin transporting Jews from Germany and other parts of Western Europe to the Auschwitz death camp. The German Sixth Army besieges Stalingrad in August; by November, the German troops are encircled by the Soviets, but Hitler refuses to authorize a retreat.

## 1943

Between January 31 and February 2, in direct opposition to Hitler's orders, the remnants of the German Sixth Army surrender to the Russians at Stalingrad; Hitler is infuriated. In April, Polish Jews attack Nazi soldiers in the Warsaw Ghetto uprising. In May, the Allies defeat the Germans in Africa. British and American troops land on Sicily in July, forcing the Germans to flee. Italy surrenders to the Allies on September 8.

## 1944

On June 6, the Allies invade Europe, landing on the Normandy coast of France. The Russians begin a major offensive against the German army on June 22. On July 20, several German military officers attempt to kill Hitler with a time bomb; Hitler survives the blast but sustains numerous injuries. The Allies liberate Paris in August and cross into Germany in September. Hitler launches the Ardennes Offensive (also called the Battle of the Bulge) on December 16 in an unsuccessful attempt to stop the Allies.

## 1945

In mid-January, the Russians invade eastern Germany; they liberate Auschwitz on January 27. Hitler gives his last radio speech on January 30 and reviews his last military parade on March 20. The Battle of Berlin starts on April 16. Hitler makes his last public appearance on his birthday, April 20. By April 25, Berlin is completely surrounded by the Russian army. Hitler marries Eva Braun on April 29, then composes his last will and testament. On April 30, Hitler and his wife commit suicide in Berlin. The Germans surrender unconditionally to the Allies on May 7.

# FOR FURTHER RESEARCH

## ORIGINAL DOCUMENTS AND MEMOIRS BY OR CONCERNING ADOLF HITLER

Norman H. Baynes, ed., *The Speeches of Adolf Hitler, April 1922–August 1939*, 2 vols. New York: Oxford University Press, 1942.

Max Domarus, ed., *Hitler: Speeches and Proclamations, 1932–1945*, 4 vols., trans. Chris Wilcox and Mary Fran Gilbert. Wauconda, IL: Bolchazy-Carducci, 1998.

Felix Gilbert, ed., *Hitler Directs His War: The Secret Records of His Daily Military Conferences.* New York: Oxford University Press, 1950.

Ernst Hanfstaengl, *Unheard Witness.* Philadelphia: J.B. Lippincott, 1957.

Adolf Hitler, *Mein Kampf,* trans. Ralph Manheim. Boston: Houghton Mifflin, 1943.

*Hitler's Secret Book,* trans. Salvator Attanasio. New York: Grove Press, 1961.

*Hitler's Table Talk, 1941–44: His Private Conversations,* trans. Norman Cameron and R.H. Stevens. London: Weidenfeld and Nicolson, 1953.

August Kubizek, *The Young Hitler I Knew,* trans. E.V. Anderson. Boston: Houghton Mifflin, 1955.

Walter C. Langer, *The Mind of Adolf Hitler: The Secret Wartime Report.* New York: New American Library, 1972.

Werner Maser, ed., *Hitler's Letters and Notes,* trans. Arnold Pomerans. New York: Harper & Row, 1973.

Paul Schmidt, *Hitler's Interpreter,* ed. R.H.C. Steed. New York: Macmillan, 1951.

Percy Ernst Schramm, *Hitler: The Man and the Military*

*Leader*, trans. and ed. Donald S. Detwiler. Chicago: Quadrangle Books, 1971.

Otto Strasser, *Hitler and I*, trans. Gwenda David and Eric Mosbacher. Boston: Houghton Mifflin, 1940.

## BIOGRAPHIES OF ADOLF HITLER AND STUDIES OF HIS PERSONALITY

Ken Anderson, *Hitler and the Occult*. Amherst, NY: Prometheus Books, 1995.

Rudolph Binion, *Hitler Among the Germans*. New York: Elsevier, 1976.

Norbert Bromberg and Verna Volz Small, *Hitler's Psychopathology*. New York: International Universities Press, 1983.

Alan Bullock, *Hitler: A Study in Tyranny*. New York: Harper & Row, 1962.

Eugene Davidson, *The Making of Adolf Hitler: The Birth and Rise of Nazism*. Columbia: University of Missouri Press, 1997.

——, *The Unmaking of Adolf Hitler*. Columbia: University of Missouri Press, 1996.

James P. Duffy, *Hitler Slept Late and Other Blunders That Cost Him the War*. New York: Praeger, 1991.

Joachim C. Fest, *Hitler*, trans. Richard and Clara Winston. New York: Harcourt Brace Jovanovich, 1974.

Charles Bracelen Flood, *Hitler: The Path to Power*. Boston: Houghton Mifflin, 1989.

Brigitte Hamann, *Hitler's Vienna: A Dictator's Apprenticeship*, trans. Thomas Thornton. New York: Oxford University Press, 1999.

Konrad Heiden, *Der Fuehrer: Hitler's Rise to Power*, trans. Ralph Manheim. Boston: Houghton Mifflin, 1944.

Glenn B. Infield, *Eva and Adolf*. New York: Grosset & Dunlap, 1974.

——, *Hitler's Secret Life: The Mysteries of the Eagle's Nest*. New York: Stein and Day, 1979.

Franz Jetzinger, *Hitler's Youth*, trans. Lawrence Wilson. London: Hutchinson, 1958.

J. Sydney Jones, *Hitler in Vienna, 1907–1913*. New York: Stein and Day, 1983.

John Lukacs, *The Hitler of History*. New York: Knopf, 1997.

David M. Moriarty, ed., *A Psychological Study of Adolf Hitler*. St. Louis: W.H. Green, 1993.

Robert Payne, *The Life and Death of Adolf Hitler*. New York: Praeger, 1973.

Fritz Redlich, *Hitler: Diagnosis of a Destructive Prophet*. New York: Oxford University Press, 1999.

Bradley F. Smith, *Adolf Hitler: His Family, Childhood, and Youth*. Stanford, CA: Hoover Institution on War, Revolution, and Peace, 1967.

J.P. Stern, *Hitler: The Führer and the People*. Berkeley: University of California Press, 1975.

Helm Stierlin, *Adolf Hitler: A Family Perspective*. New York: Psychohistory Press, 1976.

John Toland, *Adolf Hitler*, 2 vols. Garden City, NY: Doubleday, 1976.

H.R. Trevor-Roper, *The Last Days of Hitler*. New York: Macmillan, 1947.

George Victor, *Hitler: The Pathology of Evil*, Washington, DC: Brassey's, 1998.

## HISTORICAL OVERVIEWS OF ADOLF HITLER AND HIS TIMES

Martin Broszat, "Hitler and the Genesis of the 'Final Solution,'" *Aspects of the Third Reich*, ed. H.W. Koch. New York: St. Martin's Press, 1985.

Paul Carell, *Hitler's War on Russia: The Story of the German Defeat in the East*, trans. Ewald Osers. London: Harrap, 1964.

F.W. Deakin, *The Brutal Friendship: Mussolini, Hitler, and the Fall of Italian Fascism*. New York: Harper & Row, 1962.

Erik Erikson, "Hitler's Imagery and German Youth," *Personality in Nature, Society, and Culture*, ed. Clyde Kluckhohn and Henry A. Murray. New York: Knopf, 1948.

Gerald Fleming, *Hitler and the Final Solution*. Berkeley: University of California Press, 1984.

Harold J. Gordon Jr., *Hitler and the Beer Hall Putsch*. Princeton, NJ: Princeton University Press, 1972.

Robert Edwin Herzstein, *Adolf Hitler and the German Trauma, 1913–1945: An Interpretation of the Nazi Phenomenon.* New York: Putnam, 1974.

——, *The War That Hitler Won: The Most Infamous Propaganda Campaign in History.* New York: Putnam, 1978.

Milton Himmelfarb, "No Hitler, No Holocaust," *Commentary*, March 1984.

David Irving, *Hitler's War.* New York: Viking, 1977.

Ian Kershaw, *Hitler, 1889–1936: Hubris.* New York: Norton, 1999.

——, "The Hitler Myth," *History Today*, November 1985.

Lothar Kettenacker, "Hitler's Impact on the Lower Middle Class," *Nazi Propaganda: The Power and the Limitations*, ed. David Welch. Totowa, NJ: Barnes & Noble Books, 1983.

John Laffin, *Hitler Warned Us: The Nazis' Master Plan for a Master Race.* London: Brassey's, 1995.

Ronald Lewin, *Hitler's Mistakes.* New York: William Morrow, 1984.

Donald M. McKale, *Hitler: The Survival Myth.* New York: Stein and Day, 1981.

Johanna Menzel Meskill, *Hitler and Japan: The Hollow Alliance.* New York: Atherton Press, 1966.

Geoffrey Pridham, *Hitler's Rise to Power: The Nazi Movement in Bavaria, 1922–1933.* New York: Harper & Row, 1973.

David Schoenbaum, *Hitler's Social Revolution: Class and Status in Nazi Germany, 1933–1939.* Garden City, NY: Doubleday, 1966.

William L. Shirer, *The Rise and Fall of the Third Reich: A History of Nazi Germany.* New York: Simon & Schuster, 1960.

John Strawson, *Hitler's Battles for Europe.* New York: Scribner's, 1971.

A.J.P. Tayler, *The Origins of the Second World War.* New York: Fawcett Premier, 1961.

# INDEX